Modern Sashiko

26 Mixed-Style Sashiko Projects for Everyday Items

Minori

MODERN SASHIKO

Landauer Publishing, landauer.foxchapelpublishing.com, is an imprint of Fox Chapel Publishing Company, Inc.

Sashiko to Kurasu
© 2023 Minori
© 2023 Graphic-sha Publishing Co., Ltd.
This book was first designed and published in Japan in 2023 by Graphic-sha Publishing Co., Ltd.
This English edition was published in 2026 by FOX CHAPEL PUBLISHING
English translation rights arranged with GRAPHIC-SHA PUBLISHING CO., LTD. through Japan UNI Agency, Inc., Tokyo

Original Edition Creative Staff:
Photos: Yuko Fukui
Book Design: Motoko Kitsukawa
Patterns: Miyuki Ohshima
Editing: Ayako Enaka (Graphic-sha Publishing Co., Ltd.)
Foreign Edition Production and Management: Takako Motoki, Ryoko Nanjo (Graphic-sha Publishing Co., Ltd.)

Production Cooperation:
TERAS (https://akari-teras.com)
YOKOTA CO.,LTD (https://www.daruma-ito.co.jp)

Special Thanks:
AWABEES
UTUWA

ISBN 978-1-63981-158-8

Library of Congress Control Number: 2025946619

To learn more about the other great books from Fox Chapel Publishing, or to find a retailer near you, call toll-free at 800-457-9112 or visit us at www.FoxChapelPublishing.com.
We are always looking for talented authors.
To submit an idea, please send a brief inquiry to acquisitions@foxchapelpublishing.com.
Or write to:
Fox Chapel Publishing
903 Square Street
Mount Joy, PA 17552

Printed in China
First printing

CONTENTS

INTRODUCTION

The elements of *sashiko*—a stitching technique meaning "little stabs"—include simple techniques, the practicality of reinforcing fabric, and traditional patterns that can be used by everyone. Each will be explored throughout this book.

I have always been attracted by the charms of sashiko and even now never tire of them. As I encountered more and more examples of this technique, I wanted to create sashiko that could be used more vibrantly in daily life without being overly concerned with technical perfection. I wanted to embrace the puckering of the fabric and uneven stitches, allowing each person's individuality to shine through. With that in mind, I compiled this book.

One of the joys of doing sashiko is choosing the fabric. In this book, I used many well-worn garments and handcrafted fabrics. Handcrafted fabrics in Japan have unique characteristics depending on the region, giving them a rich texture that allows the feelings of the artisan sewer to be perceived in their product. I also believe that choosing fabrics with personal meaning that may seem ordinary to others, such as worn-out clothes or favorite pieces of cloth, can be the key to creating a piece that truly reflects the individual.

Although they may not compare to the original, I have also included examples of the beautiful forms of sashiko that can be found abroad. Indeed, there is even a theory that sashiko's roots lie in the Indian *kesa* (monastic robes). More than anything, I hope this book inspires interest in the connections that handicrafts can create across oceans and cultures.

In addition, I've packed this book with ideas for incorporating sashiko into everyday life. In a world of constant change, I am delighted to share with you the joy of sashiko, a craft that brings a tangible sense of comfort and grounding to daily living.

Minori

SPECIAL THANKS

The indigo-dyed multipurpose cloth on page 20 was quilted by the members of TERAS, a vocational support facility with whom I have had a long-standing relationship. TERAS primarily focuses on supporting individuals with disabilities or chronic illnesses by producing and selling their original sashiko products.

Because sashiko is both traditional and free-form, it's said to be well-suited to collaborative crafting that brings out the unique traits of each participant, whether it's someone who excels at expressing individuality or someone who enjoys steadily creating standardized pieces. That's why the items produced by TERAS are filled with the diverse charm of sashiko, ranging from freely and playfully stitched, one-of-a-kind pieces to refined, highly sensitive items.

In addition, we resonate with their approach to sustainable craftsmanship, which aligns with the original spirit of sashiko. Examples of this approach include the reuse of old fabrics discovered in local storehouses and the desire to create durable products that can be cherished for a long time.

When I saw the completed multipurpose cloth we had requested, I felt deeply grateful for the careful finishing of the threads, which conveyed their meticulous needlework. I was also delighted to discover that the subtle irregularities in the stitching, caused by the involvement of multiple sewers, created a beautiful play of light and shadow, adding even more depth to the piece.

ABOUT THIS BOOK

When we think of sashiko, we often picture beautiful, traditional Japanese patterns stitched neatly onto indigo fabric. However, in recent years, sashiko from countries like India and South Korea has appeared in stores, and a lifestyle incorporating sashiko has been spreading more widely into our everyday lives. For those of us familiar with Japanese sashiko, these international variations may seem unfamiliar but are surprisingly easy to embrace. This book proposes a new type of sashiko that incorporates elements of sashiko from all over the world. The chapters are arranged by technique and style, with an underlying emphasis on the basic concept of straight stitch sashiko.

Chapter 1: Kantha Style

Kantha refers to fabric made by layering multiple pieces of cloth, often worn-out saris, and stitching them together. It is a form of embroidery that has been passed down in the Bengal regions of India and Bangladesh. Variations of kantha include *Ralli* quilts, made by simply layering fabric and using running stitches, and *nakshi* kantha quilts, in which embroidered patterns are filled in with dense stitching.

Chapter 2: Yao Style

The Yao are an ethnic minority living in southern China and northern parts of Southeast Asia, such as Thailand and Laos. They are known for their beautifully embroidered traditional clothing. Their sashiko features include randomly placed stitches and distinctive floral and star-shaped patterns.

Chapter 3: Simple Sashiko

This style of sashiko uses simple stitches to create patterns. With no set rules, it includes many modern designs with stitches sewn straight or randomly placed.

Chapter 4: Horizontal Stitching

This technique is commonly seen in Yuza sashiko from Yamagata. Patterns are created by stitching horizontally, one row at a time, without counting the weft. There are no reference drawings in Yuza sashiko. Instead, stitching is done freely, based on the size of one's own stitches. However, reference patterns are included in the book as a guide for you.

Chapter 5: Hitomezashi (One-Stitch Grid Sashiko)

This style involves stitching along a grid to fill the fabric with geometric patterns. Because the stitches follow a consistent direction (vertically, horizontally, or diagonally), it has a regular rhythm, making it easy to continue stitching once you've learned the pattern.

Sashiko originally emerged during a time when fabric was precious, as it was a way of avoiding waste by layering cloth or reinforcing worn areas with stitching. Similar forms of stitching can be found around the world, with traditional designs and techniques passed down through generations. Even in an age when fabric is easily accessible, there is still something captivating about the decorative beauty, tactile charm, and aesthetic sensibility of sashiko. It doesn't matter whether you stitch on new fabric or repurposed, well-worn cloth. While some of the projects in this book have set sizes and include pattern templates, please feel free to customize them to suit your own taste. I hope you enjoy sewing with relaxed, carefree stitching by changing the sizes and mixing and matching different cloths and threads.

The Sashiko Featured in this Book

India, Bangladesh . . . . Kantha style

China, Laos, Thailand . . . . Yao style

Japan . . . . Sashiko traditions preserved in various regions

Japan's Three Major Sashiko Styles

Tsugaru region, Aomori Prefecture . . . Kogin-Sashi

Nanbu region, Aomori Prefecture . . . Hishi-Sashi

Shonai region, Yamagata Prefecture . . Shonai sashiko (Yuza sashiko)

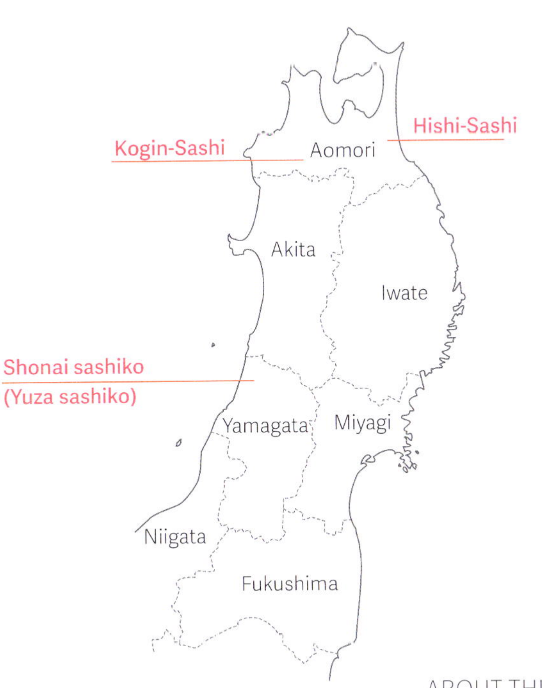

NEEDLES AND THREAD

As long as you use sashiko thread and sashiko needles, work with the options you like.

Needles

Choose the needle length and thickness depending on the thread and fabric that you're using. If you're reusing fabric, such as a shirt, the weave tends to be fine, so a finer needle is recommended. Instructions on how to thread the needle are on page 11, and having a needle threader is helpful.

Thread

Use both fine and medium thickness sashiko thread. There are floss options with a wide range of colors and skeins that come in larger quantities. Please choose according to your preferences. When stitching large projects, use skeins. When applying colors on small items, use carded floss. This book also uses regular sewing thread and embroidery thread for sashiko.

How to Handle a Skein

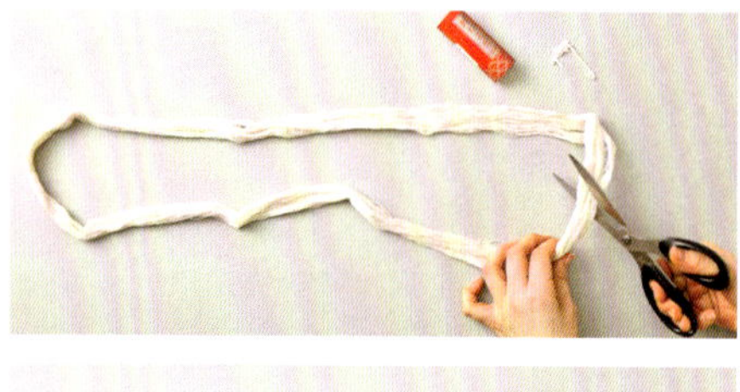

1 Remove the label and spread out the skein to prevent tangling. Since the ends of the thread are tied together in a loop, cut the knot and then cut through all the loops at that spot.

2 Thread the label back on, fold the skein in half, and tie it in two places with thread. When using it, pull the thread from the looped end.

FABRIC

When stitching dish towels, *sarashi* (bleached cotton) is typically used, but this book features a variety of fabrics. Before using the fabric, soak it in water, and if it's distorted, use an iron to straighten the grain of the fabric.

A. *Aizu* Cotton

A traditional craft of Fukushima Prefecture, this thick fabric pairs well with sashiko. It is used in projects like the needle book on page 36.

B. Vintage Fabric

This indigo-dyed vintage fabric has a unique color and texture that comes from being used and washed many times. It is used in projects like the coasters on pages 16–17.

C. Hand-Spun, Hand-Woven Fabric

Includes fabrics from the Lanten (also called Yao) ethnic group in Laos, khadi cotton from India, and cloth made from indigenous cotton varieties. I buy them whenever I come across them. Unlike industrial products, their irregularities add to their charm. They are used in projects like the wall hanging on page 72.

D. Block Prints

Indian block prints feature exotic floral designs and uniquely charming imperfections in the print alignment. They are used in projects like the drawstring bag on page 23.

E. Recycled Fabric

I also repurpose worn-out tote bags, stoles, and clothes. Some of the recycled fabrics may be harder to stitch on, but making good use of old fabric lies at the heart of sashiko. It is used in projects like the drawstring bag on page 48.

F. Kantha Padding Fabric

Scraps of double gauze or *sarashi* (bleached cotton) are used like batting. Worn-out fabrics may be used, but soft fabrics are recommended.

OTHER TOOLS AND NOTIONS

This section introduces the tools used in this book, as well as some handy extras. Feel free to use your own preferred tools and materials in your everyday work.

A. Ruler
A straight ruler with 7mm and 1cm markings is useful. I use a circular ruler when marking flower sashiko designs.

B. Embroidery Hoop
I use an embroidery hoop for Yao-style sashiko stitching.

C. Marking Pens
I use different types of pens depending on the requirements: white pens for dark fabrics, mechanical pencils, heat-erasable FriXion pens, water-soluble pens, and air-erase pens.

D. Soft Tracing Paper and Pattern Tracing Paper
Tracing paper transfers designs but leaves marks on fabric when pressed from the side without color. I use soft tracing paper, which is like a thin paper or fabric. It is more common in Japan but can be found online by searching for Adger Chaco Ace Moonveil.

E. Scissors
Make sure that you have both dressmaking scissors and thread scissors at your disposal.

F. Ring Thimble
A ring with a metal plate embedded on the side allows you to apply more pressure when pushing the needle through thick fabric.

G. & H. Sewing Needles, Pins, and Pincushion
Use sewing needles for finishing and sewing pins for temporary holding.

I. Basting Thread
Basting before doing sashiko helps prevent fabric from shifting and helps make stitching easier.

J. Awl
Used to neaten fabric edges and for cord work.

BEFORE STITCHING

How to Transfer a Design

Drawing Directly onto the Fabric

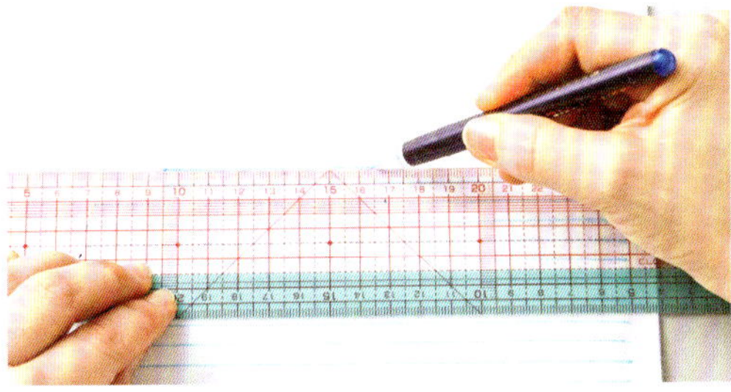

For simple designs or designs that can be drawn with a ruler, draw directly onto the fabric. Use a water-soluble pen.

Using Tracing Paper

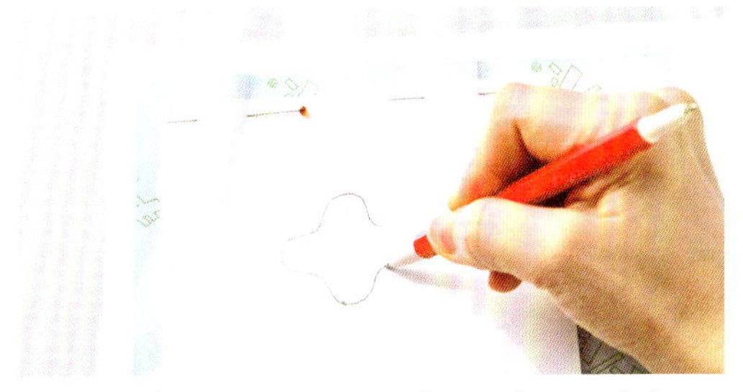

Layer the fabric, tracing paper, design sheet, and clear plastic sheet in that order, and secure them with pins. Trace the design over the cellophane using a pen (or similar tool) to transfer it onto the fabric.

Using Soft Tracing Paper

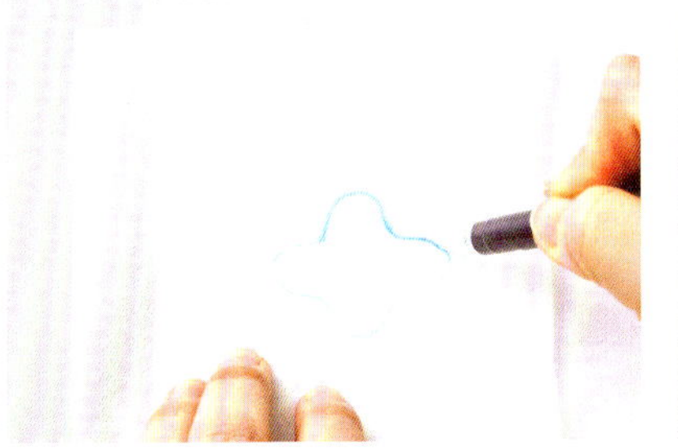

1 Place soft tracing paper over the design sheet, and trace it using a marking pen, such as a water-soluble or heat-erasable pen.

2 Place the marked soft tracing paper in the desired position on the fabric, then trace the design onto the fabric using a marking pen.

3 The ink passes through the soft tracing paper and transfers onto the fabric, allowing you to copy the design accurately.

How to Thread the Needle

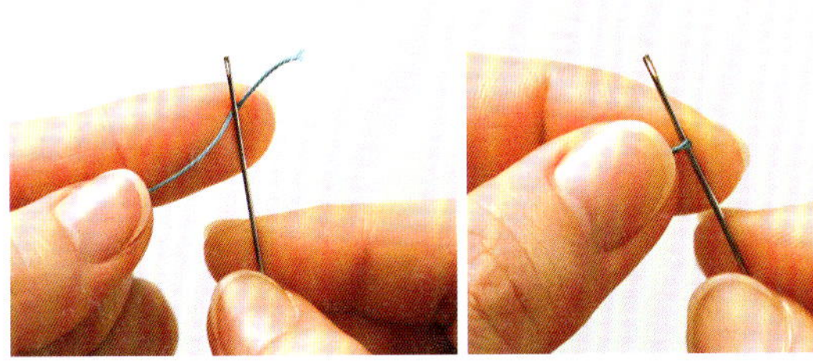

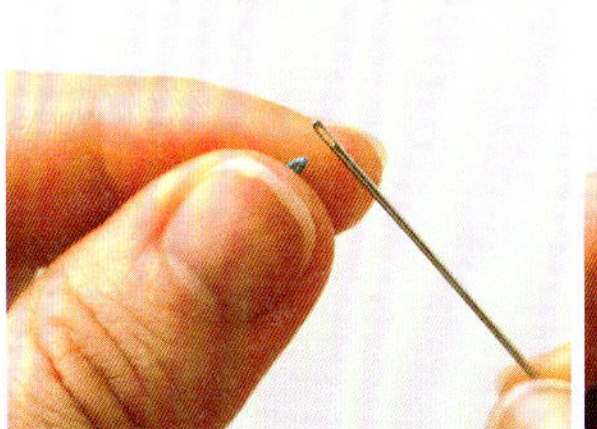

1 Place the end of the thread and the needle eye on your finger, fold the thread back over the needle to make a loop, and pinch the folded section with your fingers.

2 Pull the needle out from underneath. While keeping the flattened loop of thread pinched between your fingers, push the loop into the needle's eye. Once it goes through, pull the thread all the way through.

How to Make a Knot

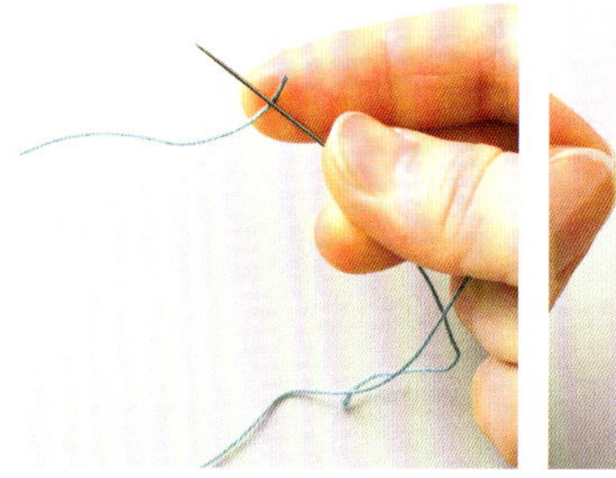
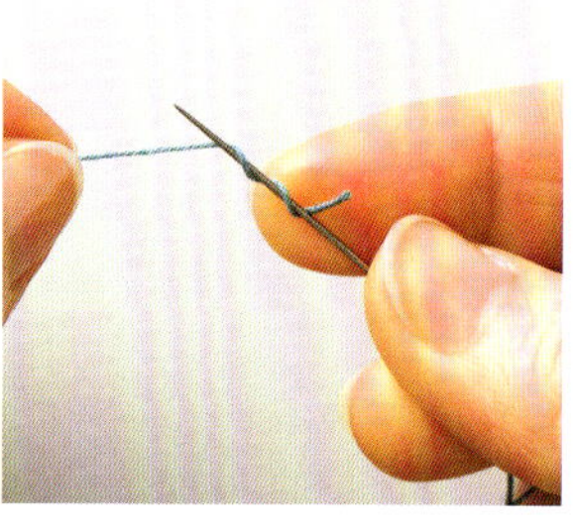

1 Place the end of the thread and the needle tip on your finger. Wrap the thread around the needle two or three times.

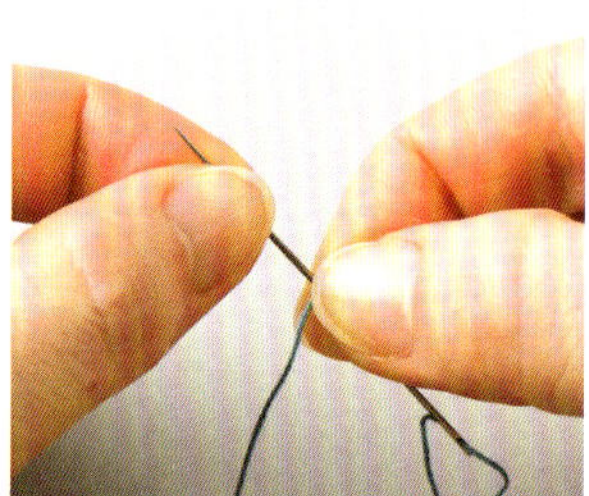
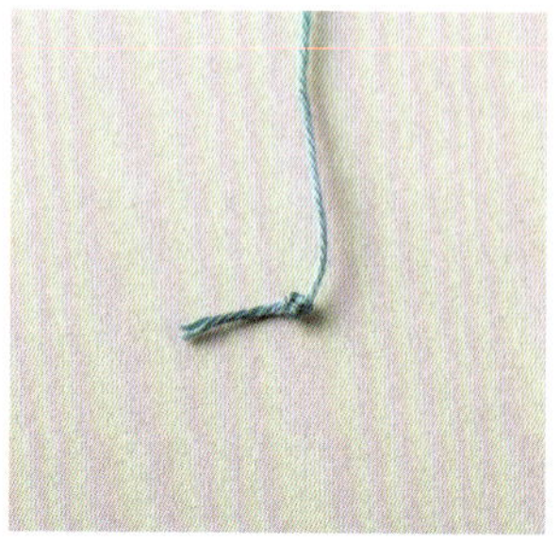

2 Firmly hold the wrapped part with your fingers and pull the needle out from the top. A knot is made at the end of the thread.

STARTING TO STITCH

Option 1: Basic Knot

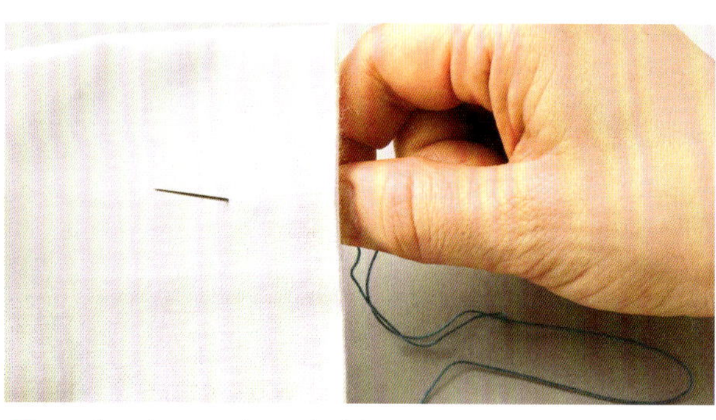

1 Make a knot at the end of the thread, insert the needle from the back, and bring it out at the starting point on the front.

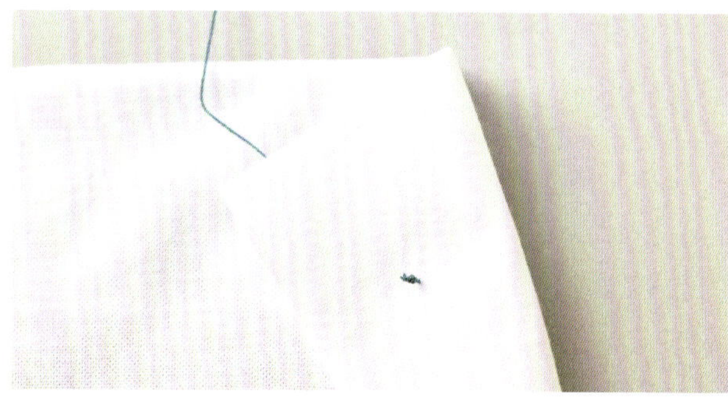

2 Begin stitching with the knot remaining on the back side. This method is fine for items where the back won't be shown.

Option 2: Burying the Knot

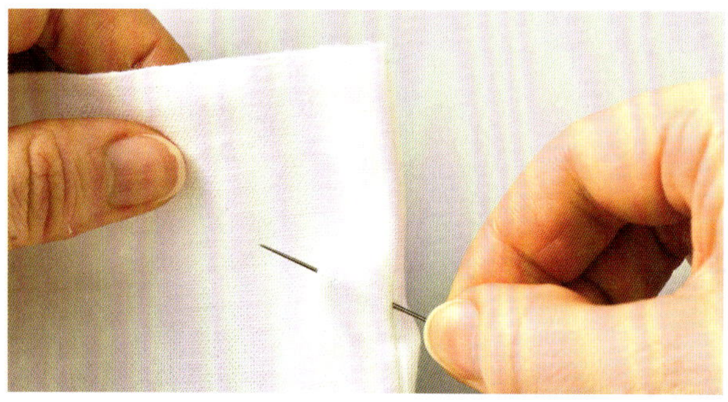

1 If you don't want the knot to show on the back, insert the needle between the layers of fabric a short distance away from where you will start stitching. Bring it out at the starting point on the front.

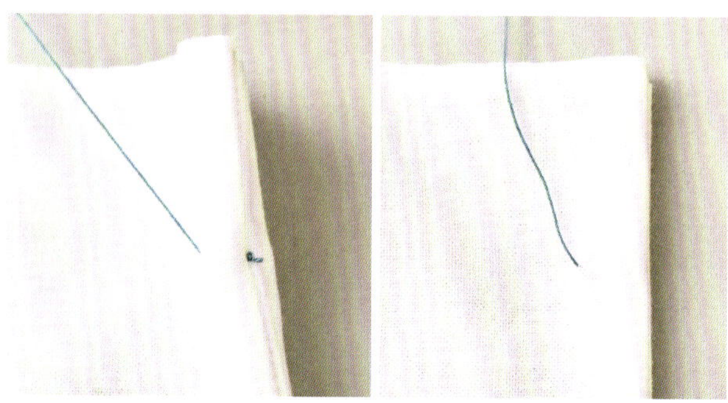

2 Make sure you have not caught the backing fabric. Pull the thread to draw the knot in between the layers of fabric.

Option 3: Back Stitching

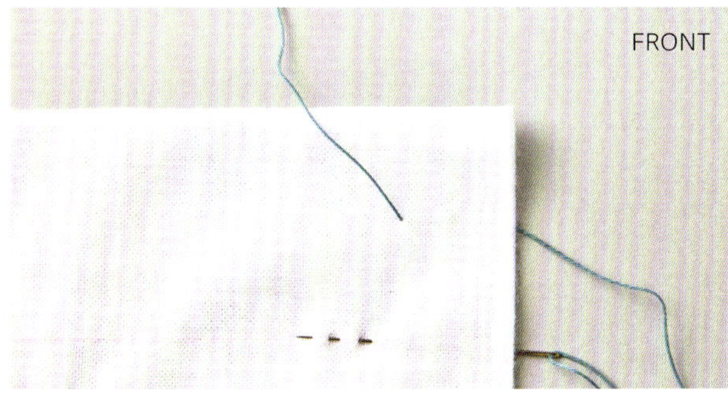

1 Insert the needle from the front a short distance away, then bring it out at the starting point to begin stitching. Leaving the thread end on the front prevents tangling on the back.

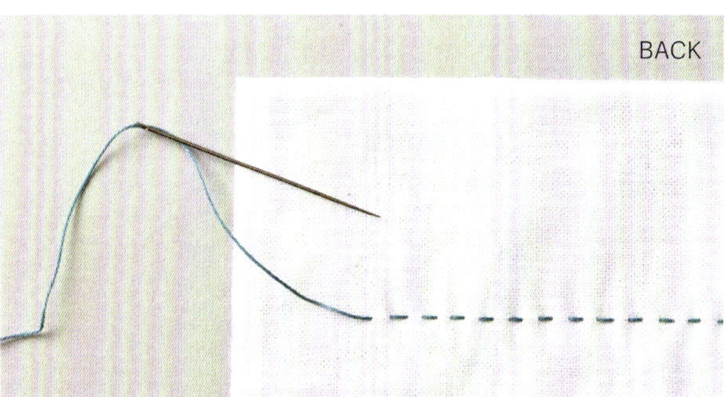

2 Once you've finished stitching, tidy up the thread ends. Pull the starting thread end to the back and thread it through the needle.

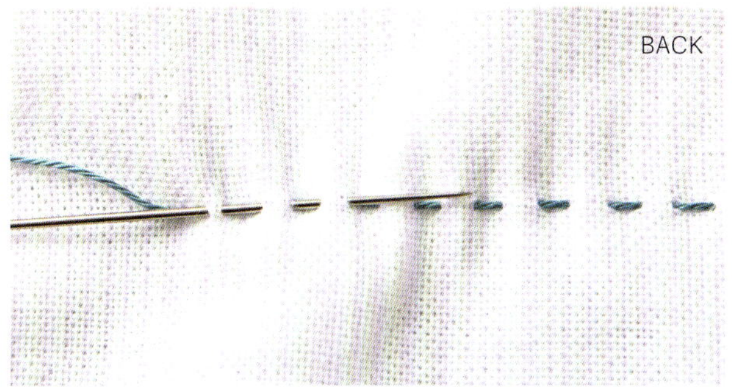

3 Stitch over the existing stitches to secure the thread. Catch only the backing fabric. Make the first stitch a half stitch, then make three to four stitches aligned with the original stitching.

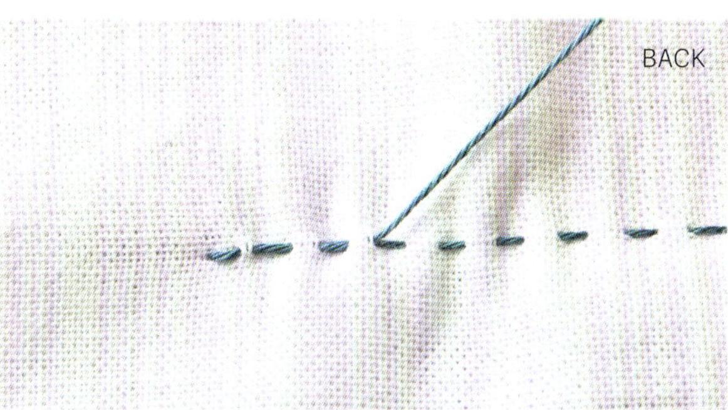

4 Once you cut the thread, the finishing is complete.

BASIC STITCHES

How to Hold the Needle

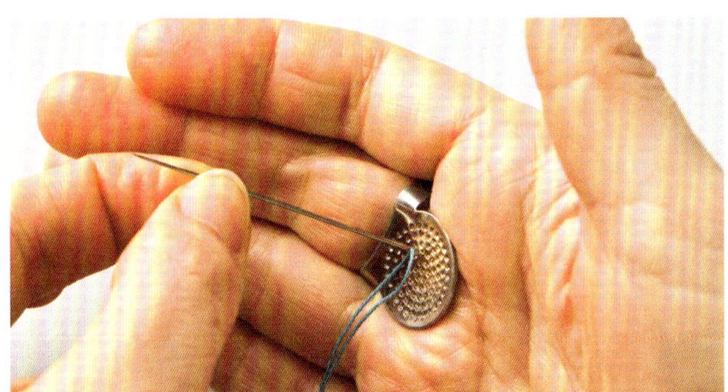

1 Place the thimble at the base of your middle finger and press the eye of the needle against the dimpled plate to hold it in place.

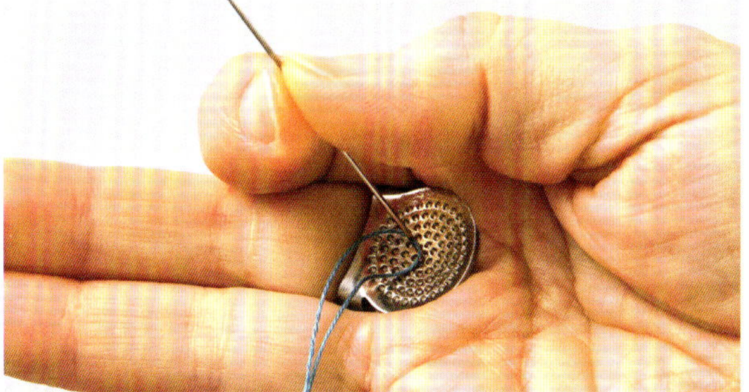

2 Pinch the needle with your thumb and index finger while keeping it in place. Stitch in this position. At first, using a ring thimble may feel awkward, but with practice, you'll be able to stitch smoothly and skillfully.

Running Stitch

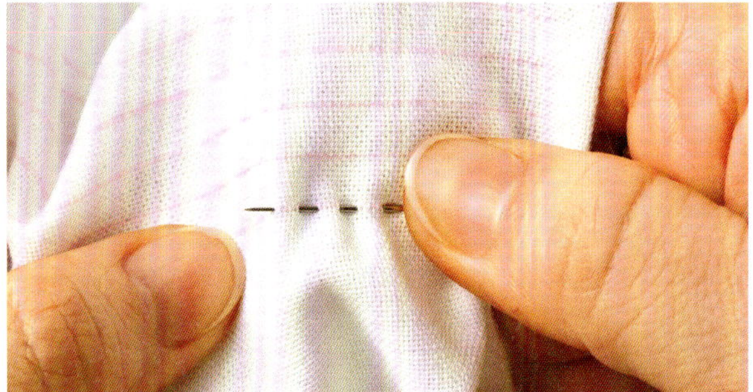

1 Start stitching by holding the needle against the thimble, and with the same (right) hand, pinching the needle and fabric between your fingers. Your left hand moves the fabric. Lower the fabric to bring the needle tip to the front.

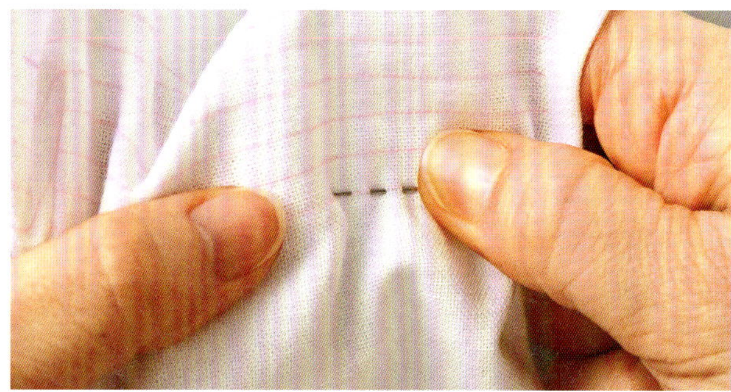

2 Raise the fabric with your left hand to bring the needle tip to the back. When the left hand moves the fabric up, the right hand moves the needle down, and when the fabric goes down, the needle goes up. This alternating motion allows you to stitch, inserting the needle vertically into the fabric.

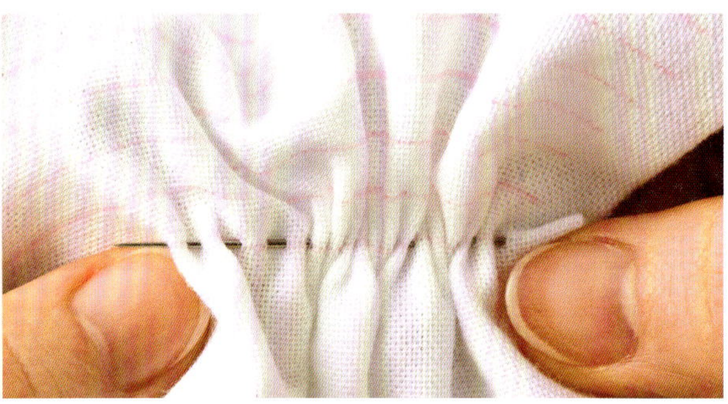

3 Instead of pulling the needle out each time, continue gathering the stitched fabric onto the needle. Each stitch should be about 2mm long, spaced evenly, or with the front stitches slightly longer. For kantha-style stitching, make the front stitches shorter.

4 When the needle is full of fabric, perform *itokoki* (thread adjustment) without pulling the needle out. Use the index finger and thumb of your left hand to pinch and hold the needle tip and fabric in place, while your right hand slides the stacked fabric along the needle to the right.

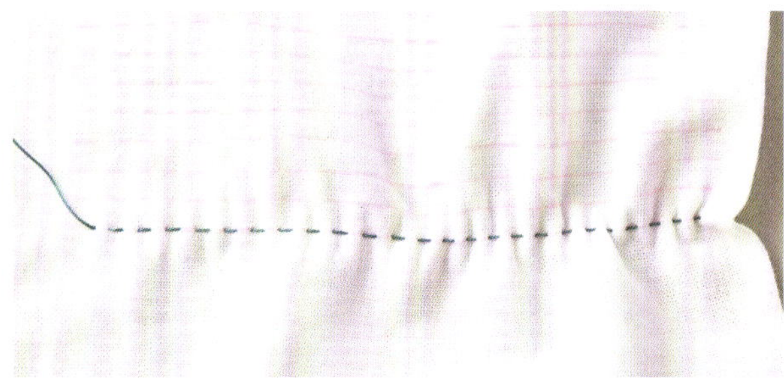

5 Continue stitching in the same way without pulling out the needle. Once you've reached the end, pull the needle through and smooth out any gathered fabric.

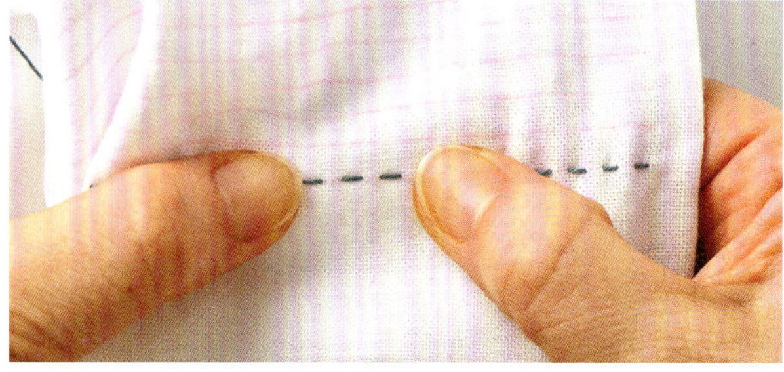

6 Pinch the stitches with the thumb and index finger of your left hand, and smooth out the wrinkles in the fabric by sliding your fingers from right to left.

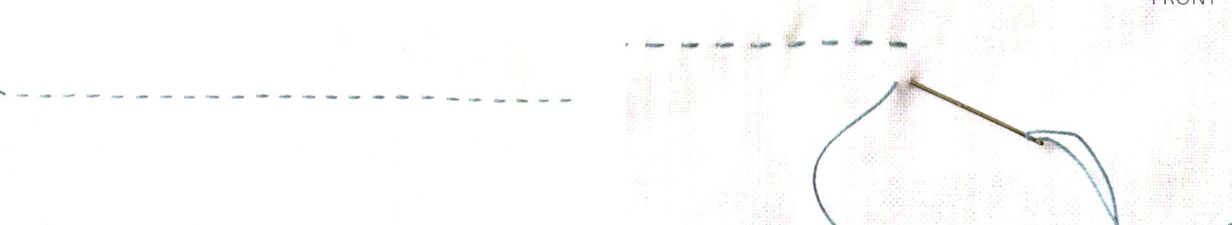

7 This completes one row of stitching. Now move on to the next row. Rotate the fabric so you are always stitching from right to left.

8 Bring the needle to the back, then bring it out at the first stitch of the next row and make a backstitch. For fabrics like kantha, where the fabric and thread tend to shift, this backstitching method is useful. However, you can also start stitching from the edge without making a backstitch.

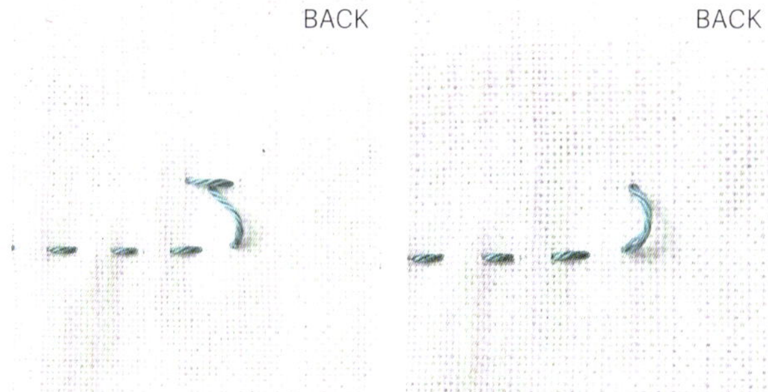

9 This is what the back looks like. The left shows the result when a backstitch is used, and the right shows when stitching is started directly from the edge.

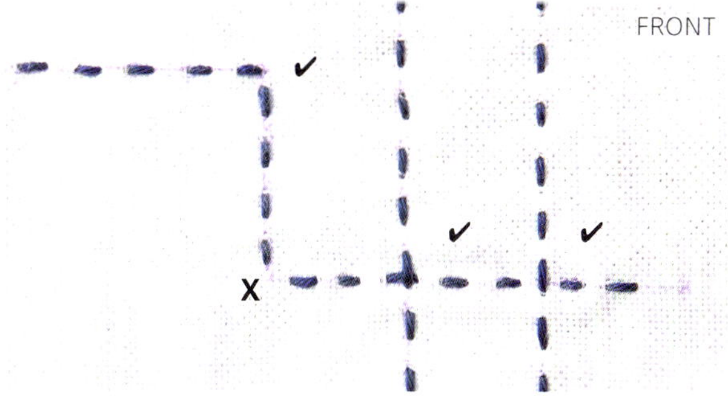

10 When stitching corners, adjust your stitch spacing a few stitches before the corner so the needle enters exactly at the marked point to create a clean right angle. At crossing points, it's fine if the threads overlap in a cross or don't overlap at all. If you want your stitches to look evenly spaced, it's best to avoid overlapping threads at the crossing points.

FINISHING A STITCH

Option 1: Back Stitching

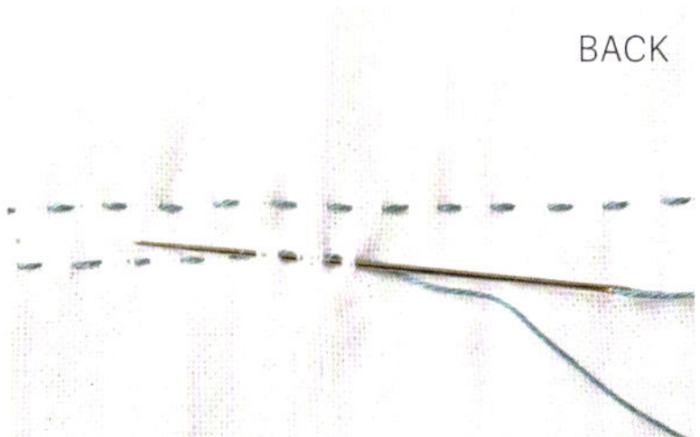

As covered in Starting to Stitch, overlap your stitches along the existing stitch line. On the back side, catch only the backing fabric. Make the first stitch a half stitch, then make three to four stitches aligned with the original stitch line.

Option 2: Knotting Off

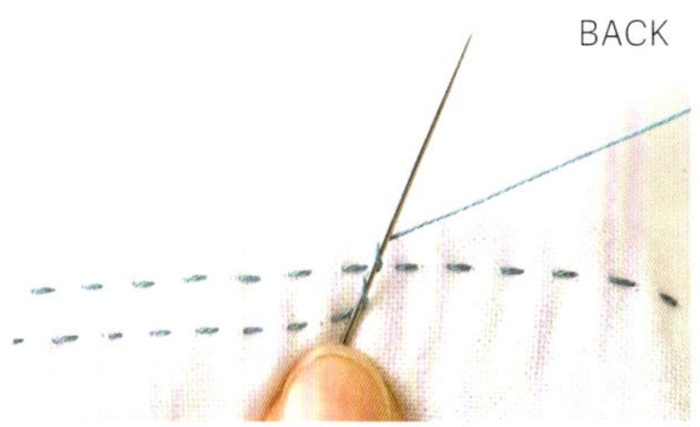

1 At the end point of your stitching, place the needle over the fabric and wrap the thread around the needle two or three times.

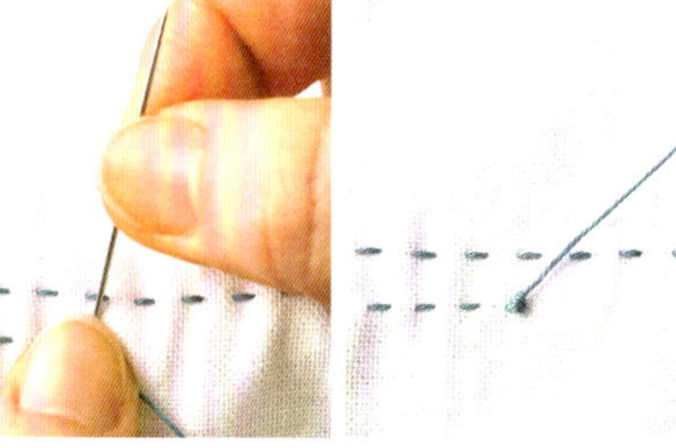

2 Pinch the wrapped thread along with the needle and fabric using your thumb and index finger, then pull the needle through. Your finishing knot is now complete.

カンタ風

KANTHA

Kantha Style

In India and the other regions where kantha originates, there are not only simple stitched pieces, but also many pieces with beautiful intricately stitched patterns. The charming, region-specific designs are truly unique and not easily imitated. In this book, a kantha-style approach is used by layering fabrics and incorporating appliqué and embroidery, combined with simple, straight sashiko stitches. Stitching across the entire surface of the fabric creates pleat-like shadows and a soft texture, giving it the warmth of handmade work. As in its places of origin, kantha-style sashiko is also well-suited to reusing worn-out fabrics.

Indigo Coasters (how to make: page 81)

The outer layers use vintage indigo fabric, while the inner layers consist of two to four sheets of double gauze or *sarashi* (bleached cotton). The sashiko thread was also chosen in varying shades of indigo to match the fabric.

Monotone Cushions (how to make: page 82)

This design is an adaptation of the traditional sashiko pattern *kadojū-tsunagi* (linked right-angle crosses). One cushion features just sashiko stitching, while the other combines appliqué with straight sashiko stitches over it.

The main fabric is hand-spun and hand-woven Indian cotton, made from indigenous cotton varieties.

Large Multipurpose Cloths (how to make: page 85)

These cloths feature beautiful shades of indigo on both the front and back. Their rectangular shape makes them practical and versatile, as they can be used in many ways.
Sashiko production credited to TERAS.

The darker fabric is indigo-dyed khadi cotton, while the lighter one is made from a vintage scarf dyed with layers of indigo and walnut. The size is just right for use as a lap blanket or a mat.

Simple Drawstring Bags (how to make: page 86)

The same white fabric used on the top bag is used on the bottom one, though it has been dyed with roasted green tea (*hōjicha*), giving it a soft off-white hue. The floral interior fabric and the beige linen are both slightly coarse-textured materials. Each piece retains the charm of sashiko while offering a different look and feel. The handle straps are chosen to match the fabric used.

To match the kantha-inspired style, I added tassels made from yarn.

Mini Tote Bags (how to make: page 87)

This mini tote is a slightly smaller size that strikes the perfect balance between charm and practicality. The appliqué is made using fabric scraps and material from bags no longer in use.

Raw-edged fabric looks cute when used for appliqué.

Place Mat with Floral Embroidery (how to make: page 88)

A small floral embroidery is stitched at the center of each grid, and white sashiko stitches are added within each section, creating a complex interplay of light and shadow. Its simple, charming look gives it a kantha-like feel.

Appliqué Dish Towel (how to make: page 90)

Sashiko stitching was added only on the appliqué and along the outer edges. The appliqué pieces are made from a well-worn handkerchief. The design is an adaptation of the *kadojū-tsunagi* (linked right-angle crosses) pattern, same as the Monotone Cushions (page 18).

The thickness of the sashiko thread varies between the appliqué and the edges.

Yao Style

This sashiko is inspired by the Yao people, who live in southern China and northern parts of Southeast Asia, including Thailand and Laos. Their traditional embroidered clothing is well-known for its intricate patterns, but there's also beauty in the more freeform styles, such as stitching circular floral shapes, stitching at random, or boldly stitching with a spontaneous, rough charm. In this section, I have incorporated those distinctive motifs into small accessories with a touch of whimsy. Unlike the orderly, refined beauty of Japanese sashiko, this style invites you to enjoy the charm of happy accidents and free expression.

ヤオ族風

YAO

Natural Pincushions (how to make: page 92)

While traditional Yao pieces often feature bold colors, these pincushions have a soft and soothing feel due to the beige fabric paired with unbleached cotton thread.

Black Envelope Pouches (how to make: page 91)

An old linen scarf was repurposed for these pouches. They were put together by bringing the corners together like an envelope. Sashiko stitching along the edge of the flap adds structure and firmness to the well-worn fabric.

These bags are just the right size to hold a postcard or a letter. The floral sashiko has a slightly three-dimensional effect thanks to the overlapping threads.

Oval and Square Cuff Bracelets (how to make: page 94)

This design features a repeating pattern inspired by stylized mineral and pearl shapes. Fill the space with swirling sashiko stitches. The combination of two different fabrics adds a unique character to each piece.

Along with an eye-catching design, these bracelets are also comfortable to wear. The red closure that fastens the loop adds a charming focal point.

Diagonal Grid Needle Books (how to make: page 96)

These needle books are the perfect size, spacious enough to hold sashiko needles. The stitches can be spaced freely, but they are arranged to make the grid pattern appear to rise to the surface.

The entire surface is stitched, like an embroidered fabric. Inside, the left side features felt for holding needles, and the right side has a pocket for holding other sewing notions

Striped Mat (how to make: page 99)

Mark only the stripe intervals with lines, and freely fill in the spaces with stitching. This version is mat-sized, but feel free to make it in whatever size you like.

STITCHING METHODS

When marking with a water-soluble pen (or similar), just define the outer shape. Beyond that, the stitching is mostly freeform.

As you'll be filling in areas or stitching individual motifs, it's easier to work with the fabric stretched in an embroidery hoop.

Stars

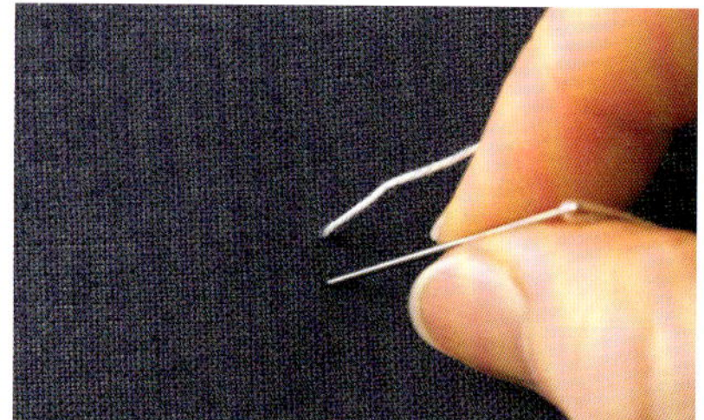

1 Stitch without drawing a design. Make a knot, bring the needle up to the front, and stitch from the outside to the center with 2–4mm stitches.

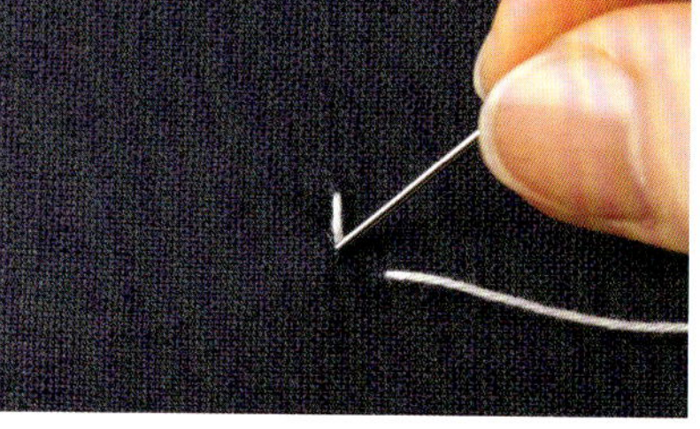

2 Next, bring the needle down and make a stitch right next to where you first inserted it.

3 Repeat this five times to create a star-shaped pattern.

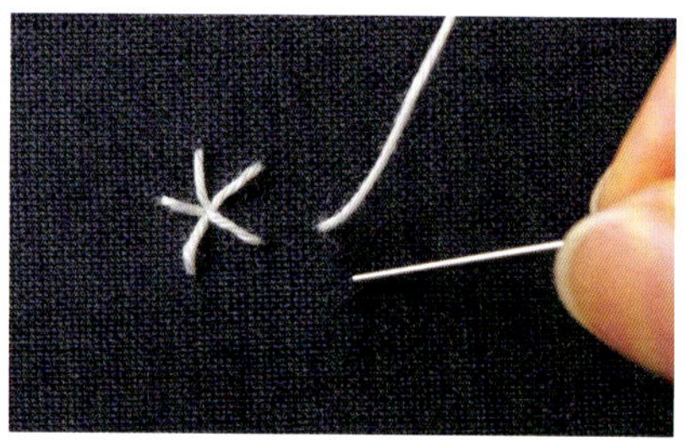

4 Continue by stitching the next star beside it. Bring the needle up at your desired position and stitch in the same way.

5 The five lines don't need to be evenly spaced. It's just as charming if they look a little playful or like they're dancing.

Seed Stitch

1 Draw the design you want to fill with stitching, and start stitching from any point you like.

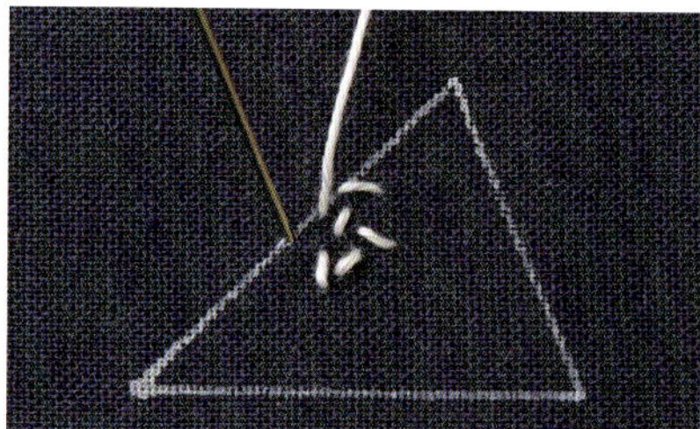

2 Keep the stitch directions random, but try to keep the length and spacing as consistent as possible. When you reach the edge of the design, follow along its outline with your stitches.

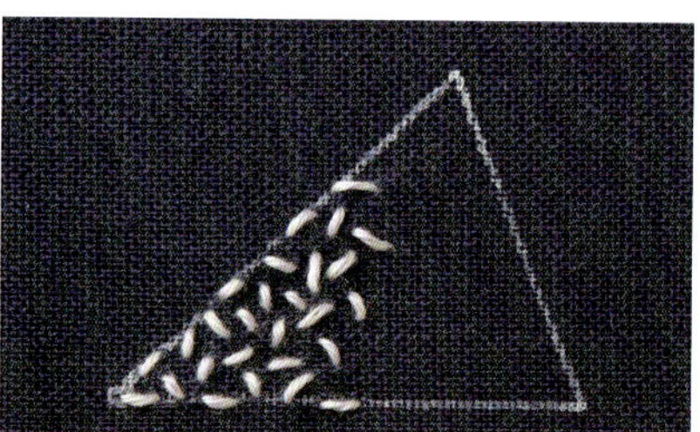

3 Continue filling in the design this way. By stitching along the outline in a few areas, the overall shape will appear cleaner and more defined.

Flowers

1 Use a circle template to draw a 1.5cm diameter circle, and mark a dot at the center.

2 Bring the needle up from the top edge of the circle and insert it at the center.

3 Stitch from the bottom to the center, from the right to the center, and finally from the left to the center, forming a cross. Next, fill in the spaces between those lines in order.

4 If the center becomes difficult to stitch due to overlapping threads, you may insert the needle slightly before reaching the exact center.

5 Once the entire area is filled with stitches, finish off the thread on the back. Pass the thread under three or four stitches on the back side, repeat this twice, then cut the thread.

6 The flower is complete!

STITCH DESIGNS AND SEQUENCES

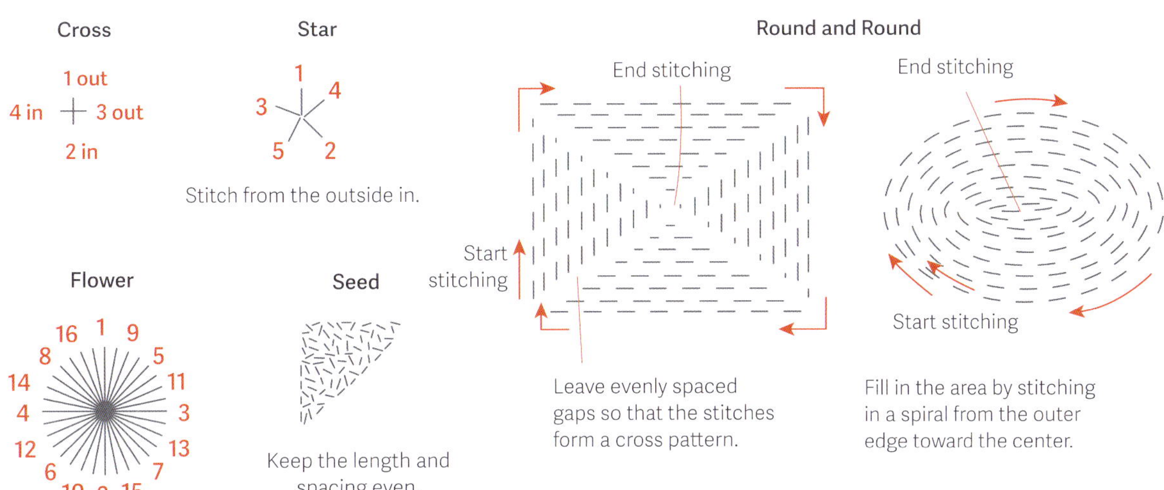

Simple Sashiko

This is a type of sashiko that uses straight lines or Yao-inspired random stitches to create patterns.

Even though it's sashiko, it also resembles embroidery. And because there are no strict rules, you can stitch a wide range of motifs, from representational designs to stripes. It's a contemporary form of sashiko that can be enjoyed in both traditional and modern styles.

シンプル刺し子

SIMPLE

Staggered-Stitch *Furoshiki* (how to make: page 100)

Furoshiki are cloths used to wrap presents. In *chigaizashi* (staggered stitch), carefully align the stitches so they alternate evenly and will give a clean, polished finish. Use two strands of thread to make the stitches stand out more clearly.

Lattice Place Mat (how to make: page 101)

To highlight the rough, textured beauty of hand-spun, hand-woven fabric, I ignored the usual rule of having to avoid overlapping threads at the points where lines intersect. There's a certain charm in stitching freely and naturally, without overthinking it.

Warikiku Envelope Pouches (how to make: page 102)

The flap is reinforced with sashiko using the ***warikiku*** (split chrysanthemum) pattern, which is often seen on old *furoshiki* cloths (cloth wrapping). You can leave a long thread tail at the start of your stitching to make a decorative tassel, or braid it into a tie cord. Both options add a charming touch.

When you unfold the flap, the full *warikiku* pattern is revealed. It's perfectly sized to hold a boxwood comb.

Modern Drawstring Bags (how to make: page 104)

Sashiko is often associated with indigo and white, but combining bright, vivid colors can give it a more modern look. These pieces were made by repurposing a worn-out shirt and a tote bag.

Top: A slightly wide, compact shape gives the bag a cute and charming feel.
Bottom: First, stitch the blue triangles round and round, then add the orange straight lines.

Reversible Cloth (how to make: page 110)

Different fabrics were used on the front and back, allowing the piece to be used reversibly. While puckering from sashiko is often something to be avoided, this piece embraces it. Stitching freely without having to worry about puckering creates gentle waves in the once-flat fabric, giving it a unique texture and character.

The starting thread is left as a fringe for decoration. The front features block-printed fabric, while the back is made from green khadi cotton—both are Indian textiles.

Various Pincushions (how to make: page 112)

You can do more than just allover stitch patterns with sashiko. You can leave pattern areas unstitched like a stencil, show the reverse side where random stitching appears, or layer fabrics and secure them with sashiko. Within each small square, there's room to experiment playfully, like a sampler.

The size can be freely adjusted to suit your sashiko or design.

STUDY OF FABRIC AND STITCHES

A. Straight sashiko stitching on *Aizu* cotton.
B. Sashiko stitches on vintage fabric.
C. Sashiko stitches over the overlaps and frayed edges of patchwork-style layered fabric scraps.
D. Grid stitching on khadi cotton.
E. Alternating two-stitch and one-stitch spacing on *Aizu* cotton.

F. Cross pattern on *Aizu* cotton.
G. Three evenly spaced stitches at a time on *Aizu* cotton.
H. Very tiny stitches on *Aizu* cotton.
I. Sashiko stitches surrounding a floral block print.
J. Circle pattern stitched on *Aizu* cotton.
K. Exploring interesting intersections on Aizu cotton.
L. Spiraling diamond shapes on *Aizu* cotton.

STITCHING METHODS

The stitching itself isn't difficult, so please take care with the borders of the design as you work.

1 Transfer the *warikiku* (split chrysanthemum) design onto the fabric, aligning it with the corner.

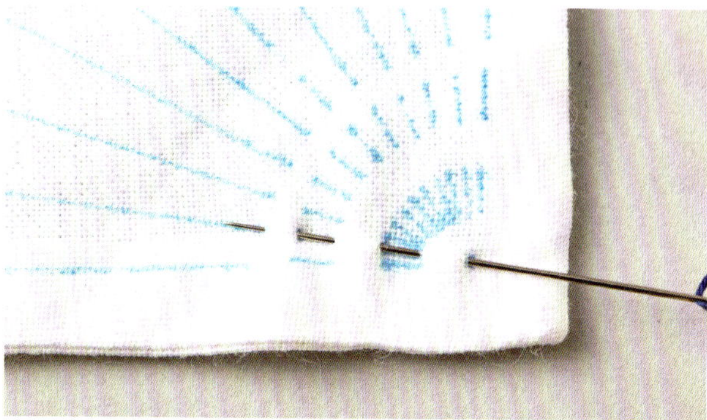

2 Start stitching from the second line in from the edge. Insert the needle at the corner, and for the area up to the second row of lines, make short, even stitches one by one.

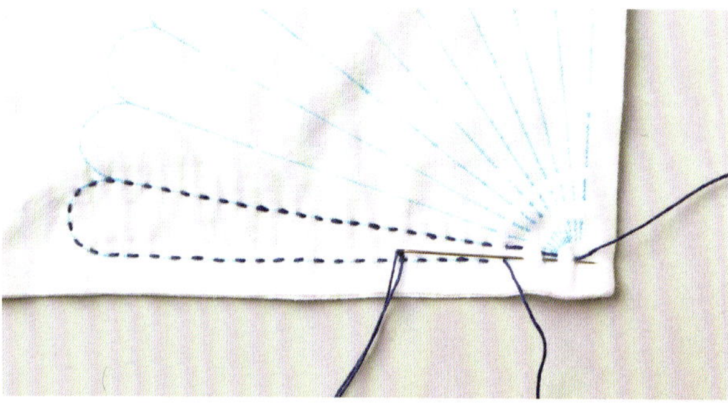

3 Stitch along the design, following the upper curve all the way around until you return to the first line.

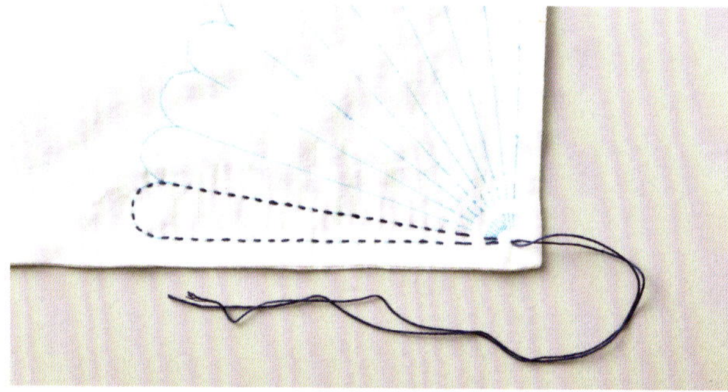

4 Don't pull the starting thread all the way through. Leave it at your desired length. This leftover thread will become the tassel at the corner.

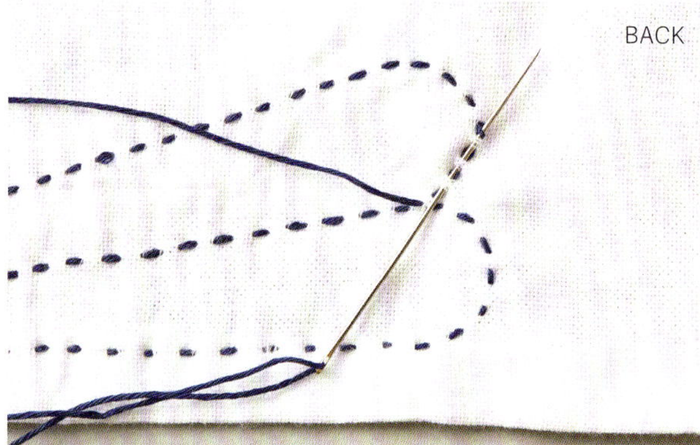

5 Stitch the third line in the same way, leaving a tassel as before. From the third line onward, bring the needle to the back at the curved section where it intersects with the edge; use back stitching to secure the thread, and then cut it.

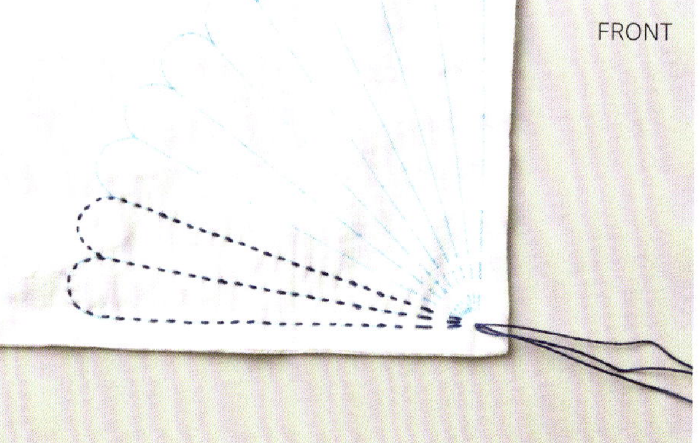

6 From the third line onward, you can use a shorter thread than for the first line, as you're leaving only one tassel.

7 Repeat this process until all the lines are stitched. The *warikiku* pattern is now complete.

8 Braid the tassels if you like. Straighten them first before braiding to keep the finish neat and tidy.

STITCH DESIGNS AND SEQUENCES

Modern Drawstring Bag (Orange)

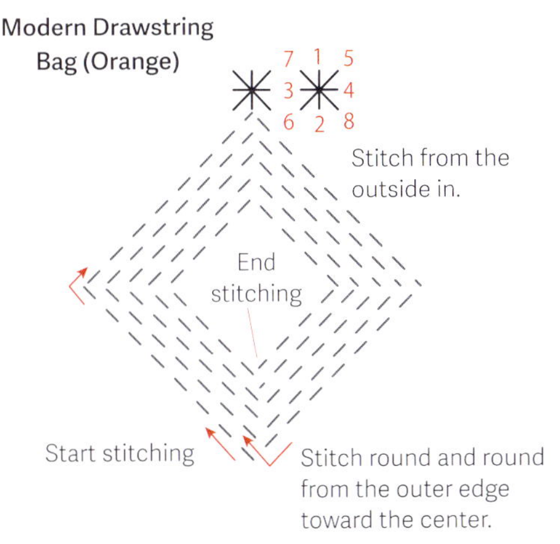

Modern Drawstring Bag (White)

Fill in the triangles by stitching round and round from the outer edge toward the center, then add the intersecting straight lines.

Warikiku Envelope Pouch

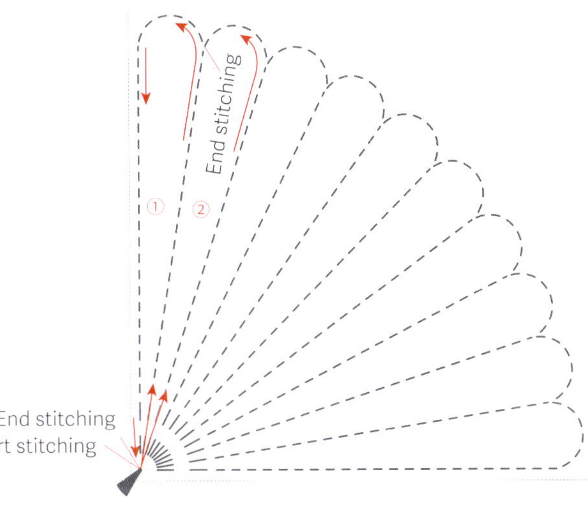

Staggered-Stitch *Furoshiki*

Begin by drawing a 4mm grid and adding diagonal guidelines. Stitch pattern ① in five rows. Next, stitch pattern ② in four rows, aligning the stitches so they alternate with those in the previous rows.

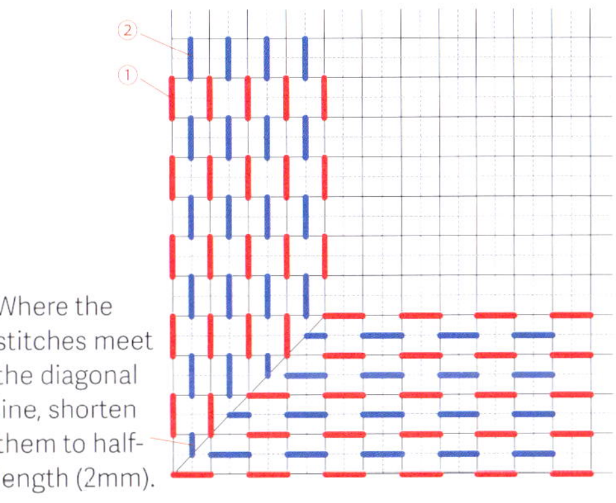

Where the stitches meet the diagonal line, shorten them to half-length (2mm).

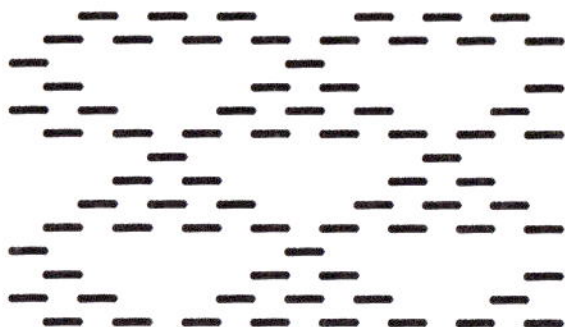

Horizontal Stitching

This is a horizontal sashiko technique seen in styles like Yuza sashiko from Yamagata. The pattern is created by stitching steadily across the fabric, one horizontal row at a time. *Koginzashi* is the same type of sashiko. However, whereas *koginzashi* follows the weave of the fabric, this technique does not. It follows the printed or drawn design instead. It's a method also found in kantha and is often used to create border-style patterns.

横刺し

BORDER

Monotone Place Mat (how to make: page 111)

A mat featuring *hishizashi*—a diamond-pattern sashiko—is made more interesting with raw fringed edges, as in traditional Indian kantha. The entire surface is stitched in a kantha-like style, with horizontal stitching added only on one side.

Triangle Sachets (how to make: page 114)

The green sachet features *urokozashi* (scale stitch), and the brown one uses a traditional *kasuri-kōshi* (ikat-style check) pattern. When the scent of the potpourri inside begins to fade, you can simply undo the hand-stitched section, refill it, and use it again.

They come with a loop, so the sachets can also be hung in a closet or anywhere you like.

Plaid Drawstring Bags (how to make: page 107)

The white pouch features a border pattern reminiscent of those found in Indian kantha.
The green pouch is stitched on khadi cotton using three strands of embroidery thread, giving it a plaid-like appearance.

The fringe also serves as a thread finish. It's made by unraveling sashiko thread to create a soft, fluffy texture. The drawstring bags on page 48 are the same size.

Sugizashi Pot Holder (how to make: page 118)

This is a traditional *sugizashi* (cedar stitch) pattern. Simple yet bold, the design stands out beautifully when stitched on just one half of the fabric, creating a striking contrast with the unstitched area.

The arrangement of the sashiko threads gives it the look of herringbone fabric. It can also be used as a trivet.

STITCHING METHODS

Stitch each row horizontally from edge to edge, and you'll see the overall pattern gradually coming together.

1 Transfer the *hishizashi* (diamond pattern) design onto the fabric, aligning it near the bottom.

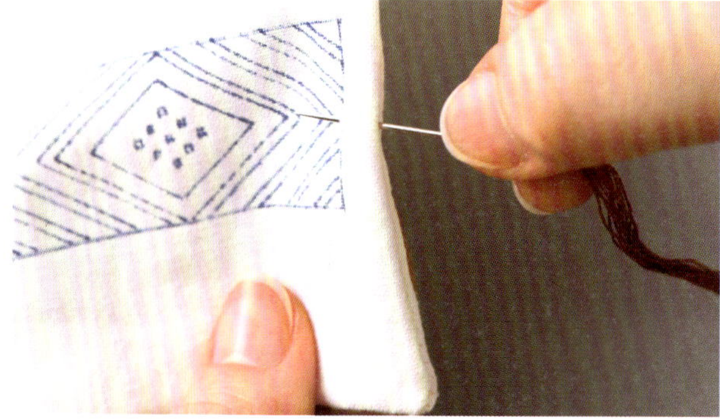

2 Start stitching from the center of the design. Use all six strands of embroidery thread. Insert the needle between the fabric layers and bring it out at the starting point of the design.

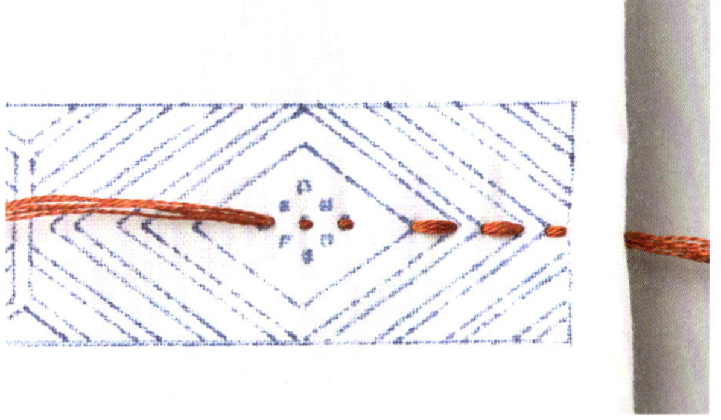

3 Leave extra thread at the start, as the sides will be finished with fringe. Follow the design as you carry the thread across the fabric. Be careful not to bring the wrong parts to the front.

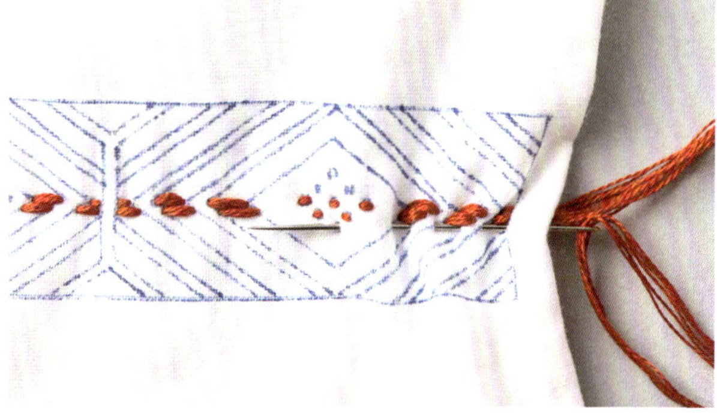

4 After finishing the first row, leave a thread tail at the end for the fringe. Then stitch the second row in the same way, working from right to left. You can start with either the upper or lower row, but in this example, the lower row is stitched first.

5 The entire lower half is now complete.

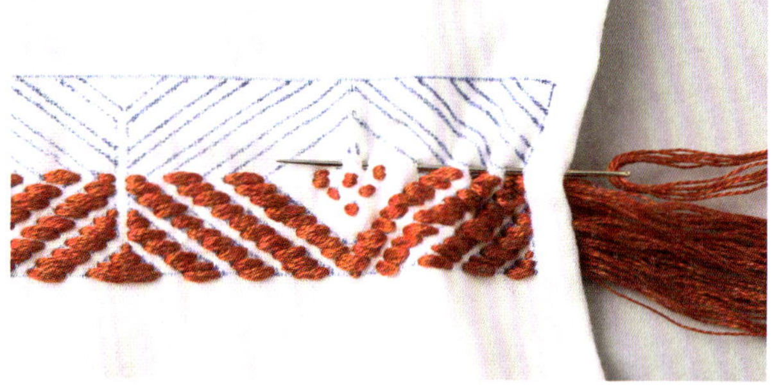

6 Now stitch the remaining upper half. Work one row at a time, layering the stitches just as before. Once the upper half is complete, trim and tidy the fringe to finish.

STITCH DESIGNS AND SEQUENCES

Monotone Place Mat

1. Start from the center.
2. Then stitch downward in order.
3. Stitch upward in order.

Triangle Sachet (Green)

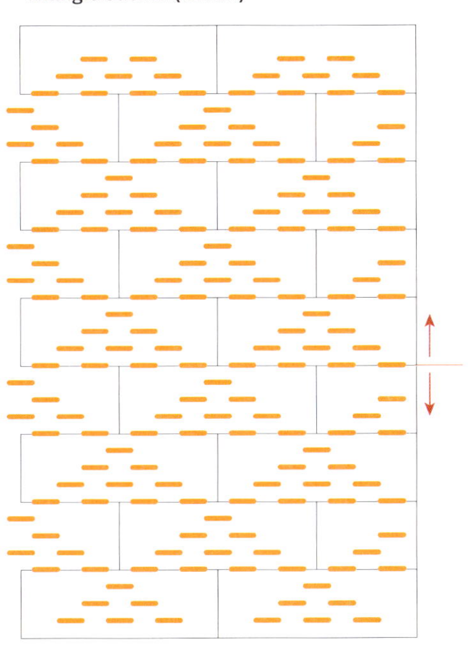

1. Start from the center.
2. Then stitch downward in order.
3. Stitch upward in order.

Triangle Sachet (Brown)

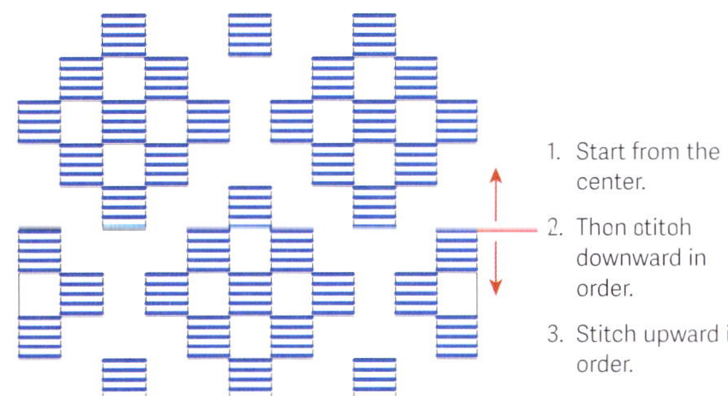

1. Start from the center.
2. Then stitch downward in order.
3. Stitch upward in order.

Sugizashi Pot Holder

1. Start from the center
2. Then stitch to the right in order.
3. Stitch to the left in order.

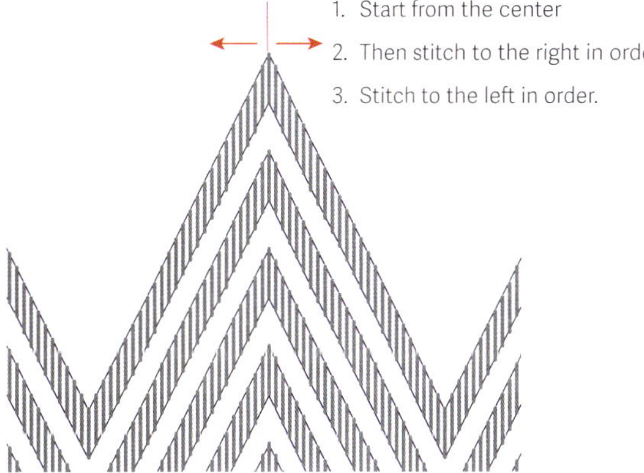

Plaid Drawstring Bag (White)

4. Start from the center.
5. Then stitch to the right in order.
6. Stitch to the left in order.

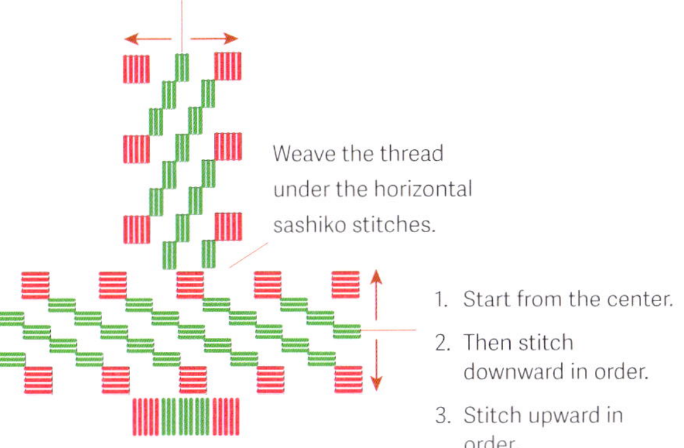

Weave the thread under the horizontal sashiko stitches.

1. Start from the center.
2. Then stitch downward in order.
3. Stitch upward in order.

Leave as a fringe.

Plaid Drawstring Bag (Green)

4. Start from the center.
5. Then stitch to the right in order.
6. Stitch to the left in order.

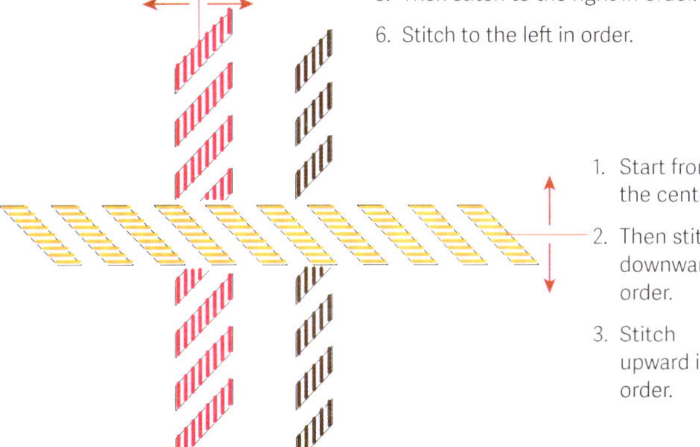

1. Start from the center.
2. Then stitch downward in order.
3. Stitch upward in order.

Hitomezashi (One-Stitch Grid Sashiko)

The pattern is created by stitching one stitch at a time along the squares of a grid, vertically, horizontally, and diagonally. Once you've stitched all in one direction, turn the fabric and stitch in the same direction again. While this technique is best known for being used in *hanafukin* (decorative dishcloths), stitched over the entire surface of *sarashi* (bleached cotton) fabric, here it's used in a more design-focused way for tapestries and mats as interior décor.

一目刺し

GRID

Indigo Mini Mats (how to make: page 120)

This piece uses vintage indigo fabric. The pattern on the mat at the back is *dan-tsunagi* (linked steps). The patchwork mat in the front, which combines various fabrics, also uses *dan-tsunagi* as a base, but with an adapted design that gives it a sampler-like feel.

Lattice Basket Cover (how to make: page 117)

This design enlarges the single-stitch grid pattern into a larger grid. The traditional motif takes on a modern look.

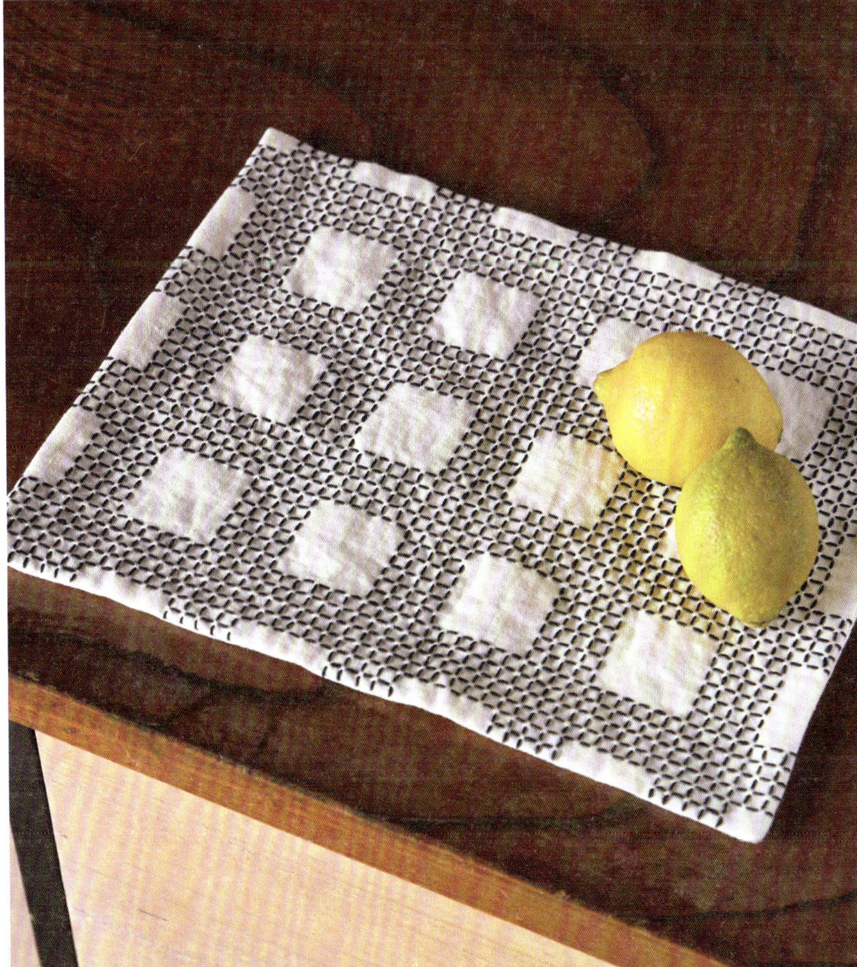

Because the stitches are made in a regular pattern, it can look like a textile. If you want to change the size of the fabric, it will look nicer if the appearance of the grid is kept even both vertically and horizontally.

Patterned Wall Hanging (how to make: page 122)

The pattern is a traditional design called *kaki no hana* (persimmon flower). While stitching the entire surface can look beautiful, adding a bit of design variation can create a sense of lightness and make it fit better with your room.

The bottom has been turned into a fringe by removing the horizontal (weft) weaving threads.

Large Wall Hangings (how to make: page 124)

I used a thin fabric and stitched only around the edges with sashiko to keep it light. The white piece combines *jujizashi* (cross stitch) and *kugurizashi* (woven stitch), while the pink piece features the traditional *kaki no hana* (persimmon flower) pattern on the border.

壁に吊るしても、何かにかけて使ってもふわっとした軽さがちょうどいい。

Whether you hang it on the wall or drape it over something, the cloth's soft, airy lightness feels just right.

STITCHING METHODS

Stitch uniformly along the grid lines. Look closely at the pattern and be careful not to stitch in the wrong places.

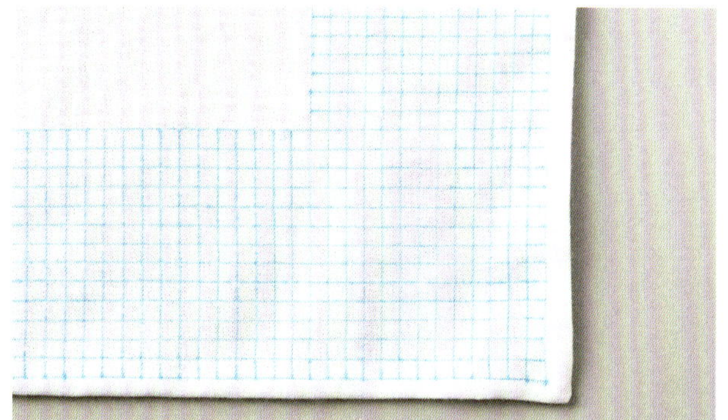

1 We'll be stitching the *kaki no hana* (persimmon flower) pattern. Draw 5mm grid guidelines on the area where you want to do the sashiko.

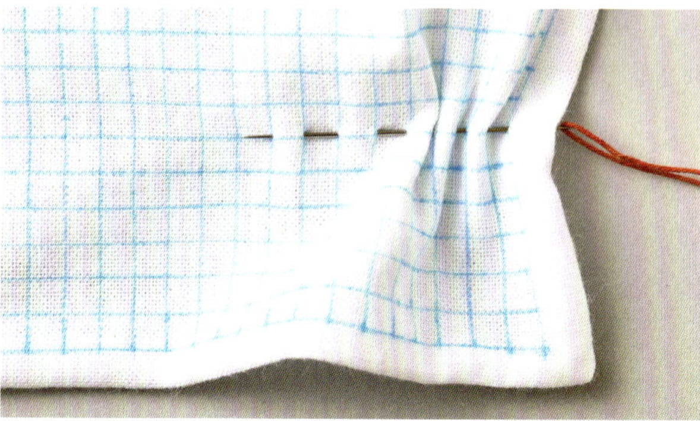

2 Start stitching from the row where the threads meet at the same position. On the back side, you can tie a knot, or if you prefer not to show the knot, you can use back stitching instead. Whichever method you prefer is fine.

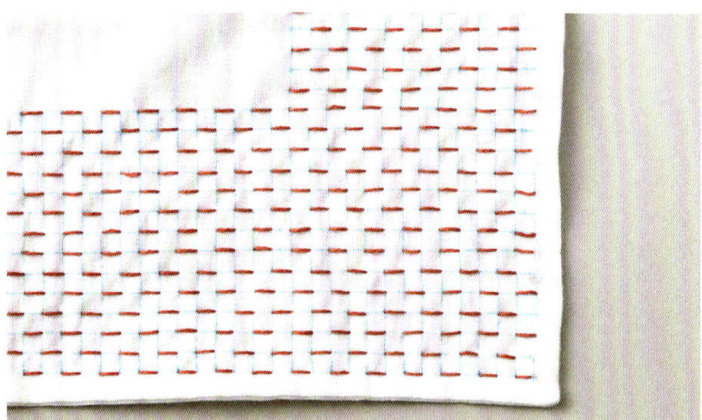

3 Follow the design and stitch only the horizontal lines. Be sure to double-check where you're stitching.

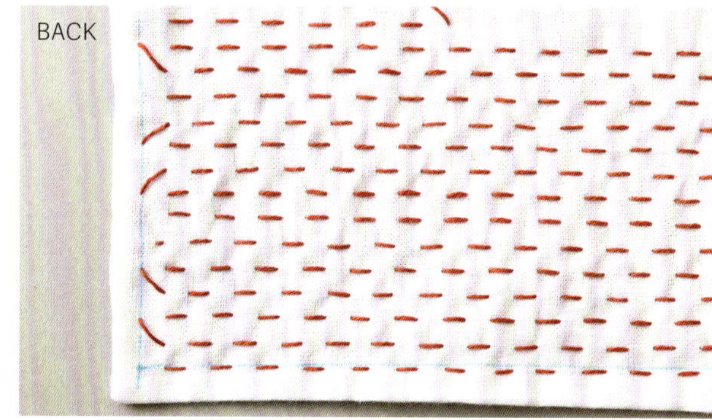

4 When moving to a new row, carry the thread along the back. To finish off, you can either tie a knot or use back stitching, whichever you prefer.

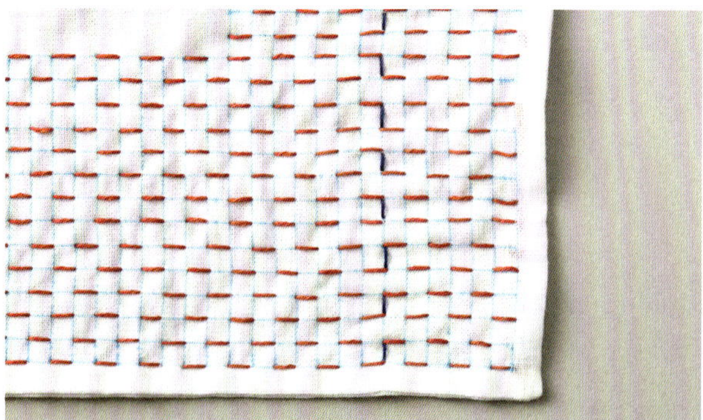

5 Next, stitch the vertical lines (You will turn the work so the stitches are horizontal, but this image is not turned for instructional purposes.) As before, start from the row where the threads meet at the same position.

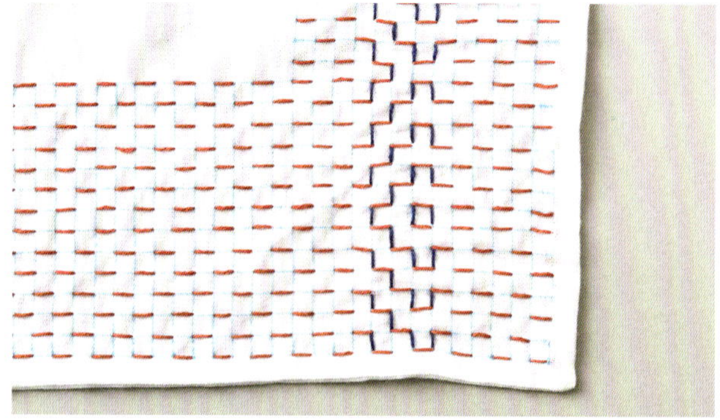

6 Stitch only the vertical lines, checking the pattern placement as you go. Gradually, the design will begin to take shape. Continue stitching this way until the end, and it will be complete.

STITCH DESIGNS AND SEQUENCES

Indigo Mini Mat (Patchwork)

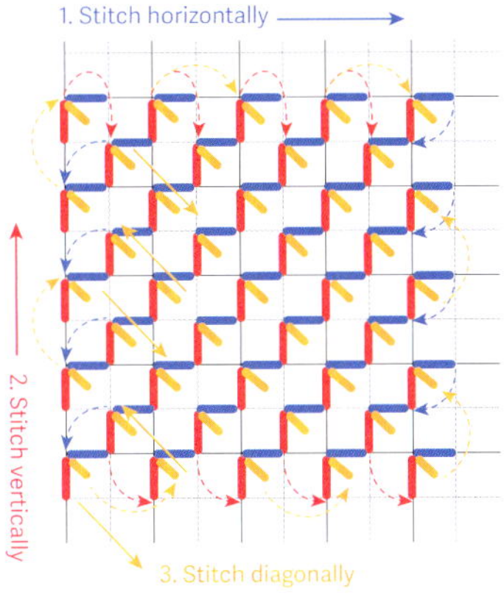

1. Stitch horizontally
2. Stitch vertically
3. Stitch diagonally

Indigo Mini Mat (Single Layer)

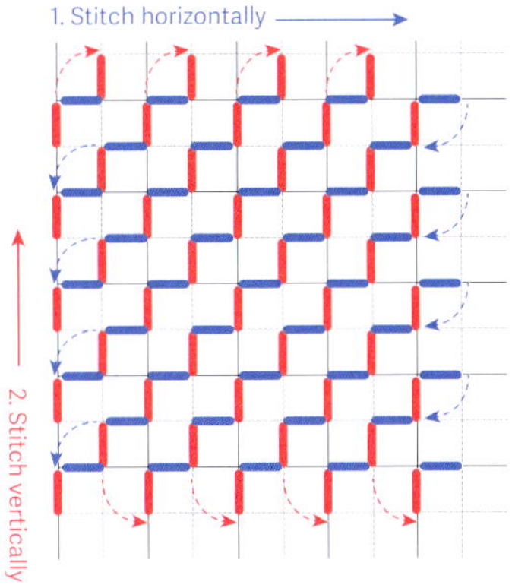

1. Stitch horizontally
2. Stitch vertically

Lattice Basket Cover

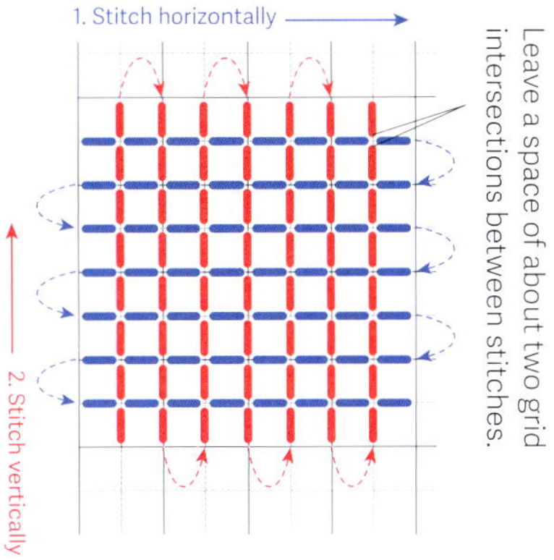

1. Stitch horizontally
2. Stitch vertically
Leave a space of about two grid intersections between stitches.

Wall Hangings

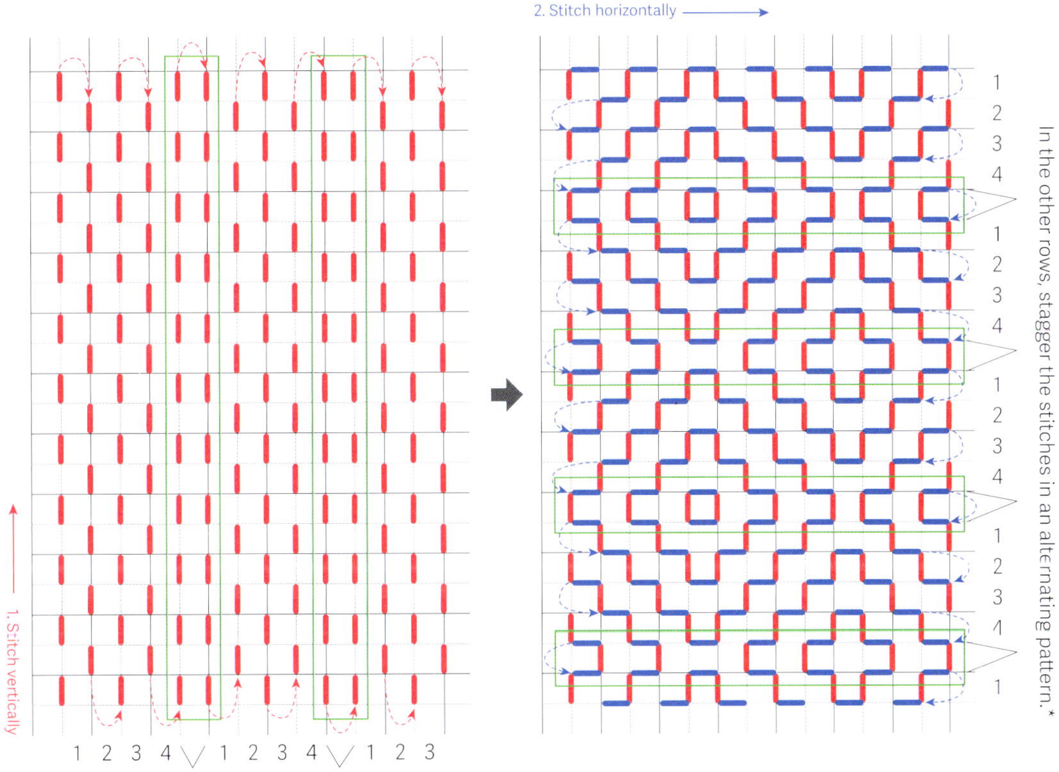

1. Stitch vertically
2. Stitch horizontally
1 2 3 4 1 2 3 4 1 2 3
1 2 3 4 1 2 3 4 1 2 3 4 1 2 3 4 1
Every four squares, the threads align and face each other. In the other rows, stagger the stitches in an alternating pattern.*

Every four squares, the threads align and face each other. In the other rows, stagger the stitches in an alternating pattern.*

*For the Large Wall Hanging (pink), stitch so that the lines face each other every ***six*** squares.

Large Wall Hanging (White)

0.3cm
1cm
Start stitching
End stitching

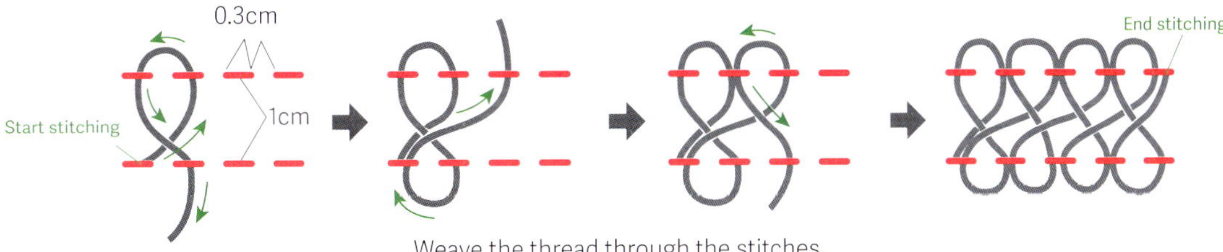

Weave the thread through the stitches.

DESIGNS FOR HITOMEZASHI

Hitomezashi (one-stitch grid sashiko) allows for a variety of patterns to be created using combinations of vertical, horizontal, and diagonal stitches. Here, we introduce hitomezashi patterns with the same 5mm spacing, making them easy to incorporate into your own projects.

Jujizashi (Cross Stitch)

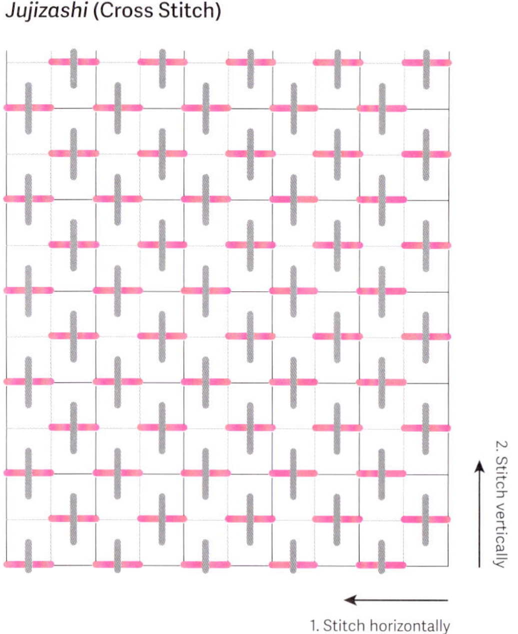

Stitch horizontally along the grid at 5mm intervals, followed by the vertical lines.

Crossed Floral Stitch

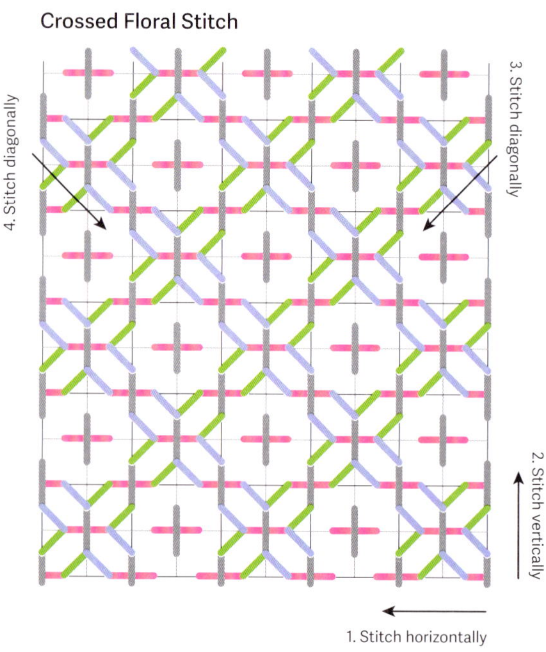

Stitch horizontally along the grid at 5mm intervals, followed by the vertical lines. After that, stitch diagonally, aligning with the intersections of the horizontal and vertical lines

Zenizashi (Coin Stitch)

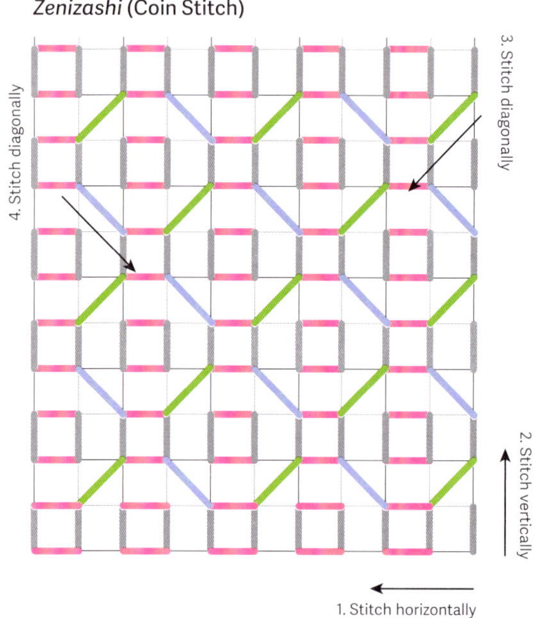

Stitch horizontally along the grid at 5mm intervals, followed by the vertical lines. After that, add diagonal stitches, aligning them with the intersections of the vertical and horizontal lines.

Rice Flower Stitch

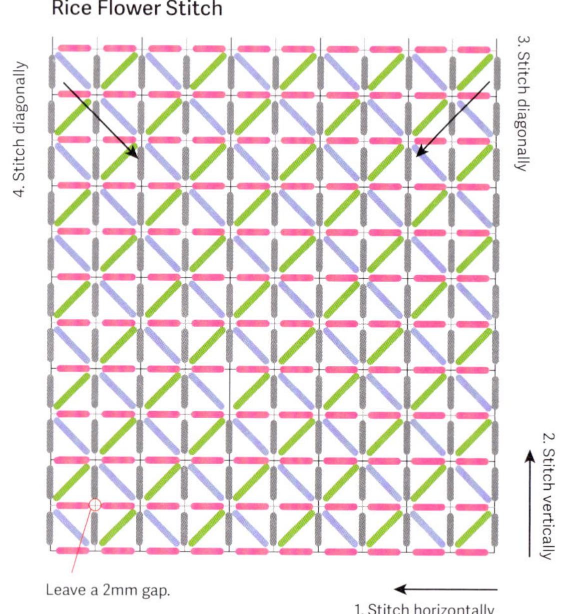

Stitch horizontally along the grid using 3mm stitches, then stitch vertically in the same way. After that, add diagonal stitches, leaving gaps for the intersections of the vertical and horizontal lines.

Floral Cross Stitch

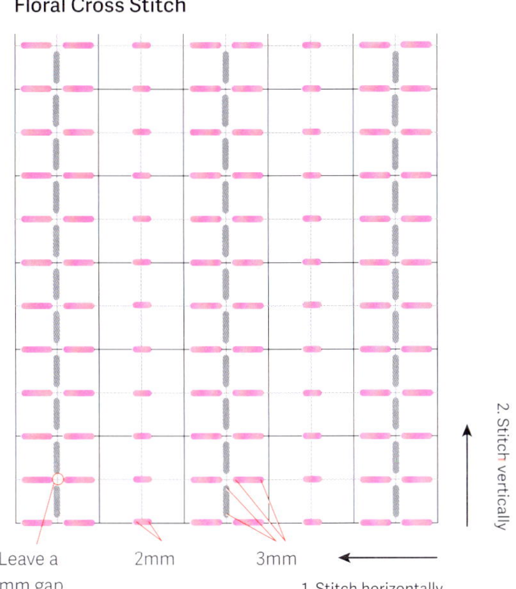

Stitch horizontally along the grid using stitch lengths of 3mm, 3mm, and 2mm in sequence. Then stitch vertically using 3mm stitches.

Kagome (Basket Weave Pattern)

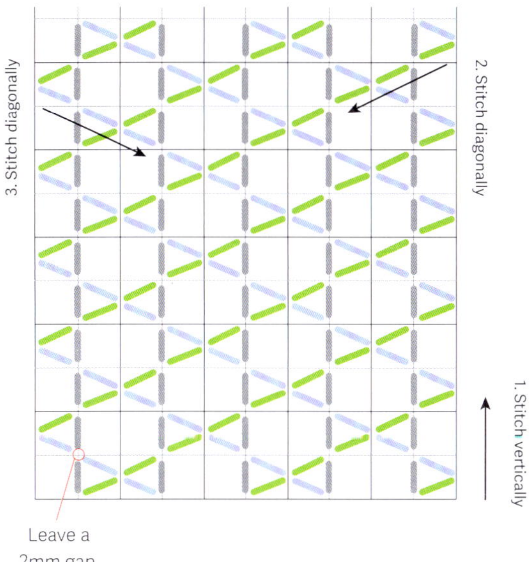

Stitch vertically along the grid using 3mm stitches. Then, add diagonal stitches.

Persimmon Flower Stitch (Fine Type)

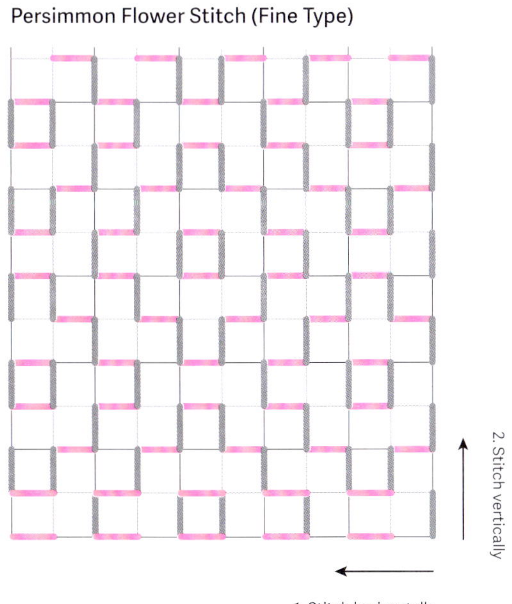

Stitch horizontally along the grid at 5mm intervals, then stitch vertically. In the vertical direction, place stitches every two squares; in the horizontal direction, place them every other square so they face each other.

Tree of Crosses

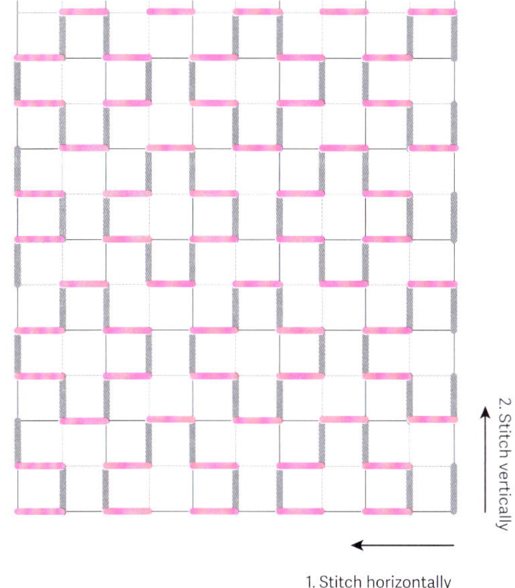

Stitch horizontally along the grid at 5mm intervals, then stitch vertically. In the horizontal direction, place stitches every other square so they face each other.

How to Make the Projects

- The numbers used throughout this book are in metric to maintain the dimensions provided by the author. All the numbers in the diagrams are in centimeters (cm).
- Unless otherwise noted, the measurements in the layout diagrams and patterns **do not include seam allowances.** As a general guideline: use a **0.7cm seam allowance** when sewing fabric pieces together, **0.5cm** for appliqué, and around **1cm** for final construction seams. If a piece is marked as "cut to size," cut the fabric **without a seam allowance.**
- Dashed lines with no specific instructions indicate **seam or stitch lines** (sashiko or otherwise).
- Fabric measurements are listed as **width × length**. Fabric quantities include a bit of extra to allow for adjustments. Finished project dimensions are shown as **height × width**.
- Since extensive sashiko stitching can cause the fabric to shrink slightly, either factor in an extra margin of error when cutting the fabric, or remeasure and adjust the size after stitching.
- The sashiko thread numbers refer to **DARUMA Sashiko Thread color numbers**. There are cardboard-bobbin and skein options, and the numbers shown are for the cardboard-bobbin type. Please note that the same color may have different numbers depending on the packaging type.
- Feel free to use any fabrics and threads you prefer.
- The finished size of the project may vary slightly from the dimensions shown in the diagrams.

PAGE 17 → INDIGO COASTERS

Finished size:
10 × 10cm

Materials (for one coaster):
Outer fabric: 25 × 15cm
Inner fabric: 25 × 25cm
DARUMA Sashiko Thread (Thin) in colors: 205 (Peacock), 215 (Navy Blue), 216 (Deep Indigo), 225 (Lapis Lazuli)

Tips:
- For kantha-style stitching, layer two to four pieces of inner fabric.
- Adjust the number and size of layers depending on the fabric used.

Instructions:
1. Place the two outer fabric pieces right sides together, layer the inner fabric below, and sew around the edges, leaving a small opening for turning.
2. Turn right side out, hand-sew the opening closed with a slip stitch, then do kantha quilting over the surface.

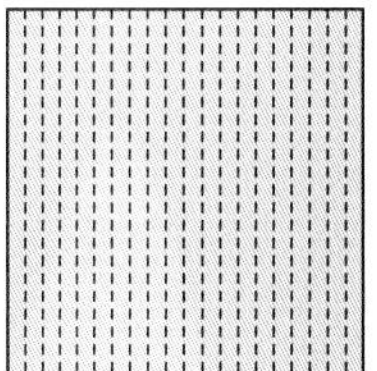

Outer Layer (two pieces)

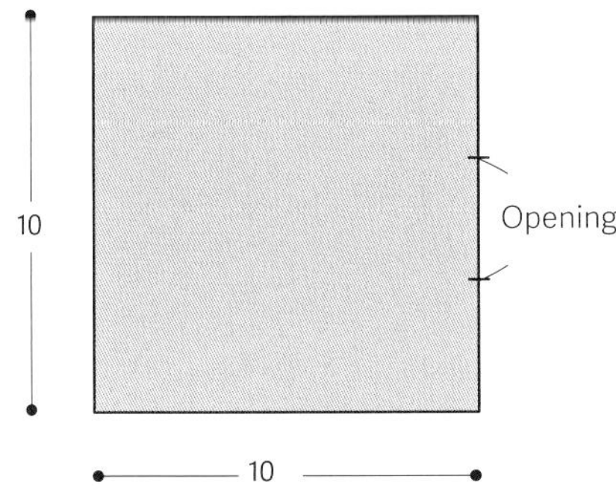

How to Assemble

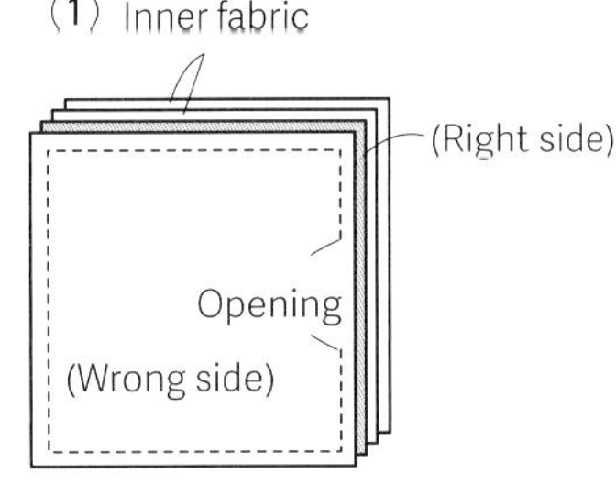

Place the two main pieces of fabric right sides together, layer the inner fabric (same size) on one side (shown behind). Leaving a small opening for turning, sew around the edges.

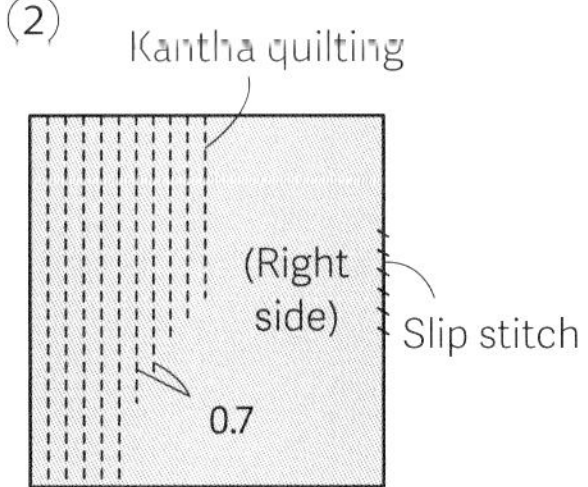

Turn the piece right side out, slip stitch the opening closed, and do kantha quilting over the surface.

PAGE 18 → MONOTONE CUSHIONS

Finished size:
30 × 30cm

Materials (for one cushion):
Outer fabric: 90 × 35cm
Inner fabric: 90 × 110cm
Appliqué fabric: 50 × 30cm (A only)
Cushion insert: 30 × 30cm
DARUMA Home Thread (Fine) in color: 8 (Cream)
DARUMA Sashiko Thread (Thick) in color: 219 (Black) (B only)

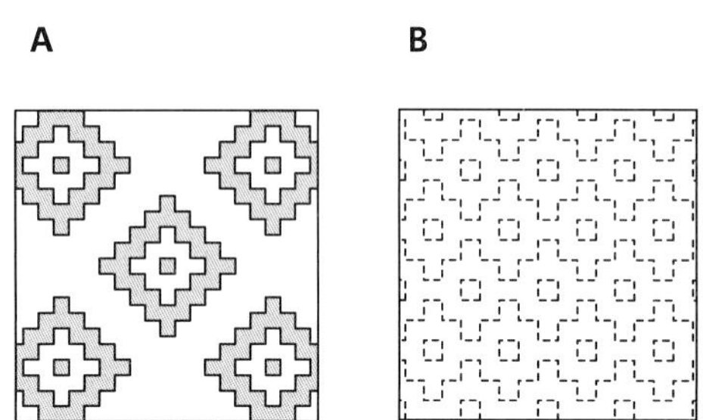

Tips:

- Use two strands of thread for stitching. Use sashiko thread for sashiko, and regular sewing thread for kantha quilting.
- For kantha, layer two to four pieces of inner fabric. Adjust the number and size of layers depending on the fabric used.
- Since kantha quilting can cause the fabric to shrink, you may want to recalculate the finished dimensions before assembling the final piece.

Instructions:

1. Add the appliqué or sashiko stitching to complete the front piece.
2. Layer inner fabric with the front piece, and do the kantha quilting. Repeat with the back pieces.
3. For both back pieces, triple fold a seam allowance at the opening end. Hand stitch it closed.
4. Place the front and back pieces right sides together (overlap the back pieces as needed), and sew around the edges.
5. Turn right side out. Insert the cushion.

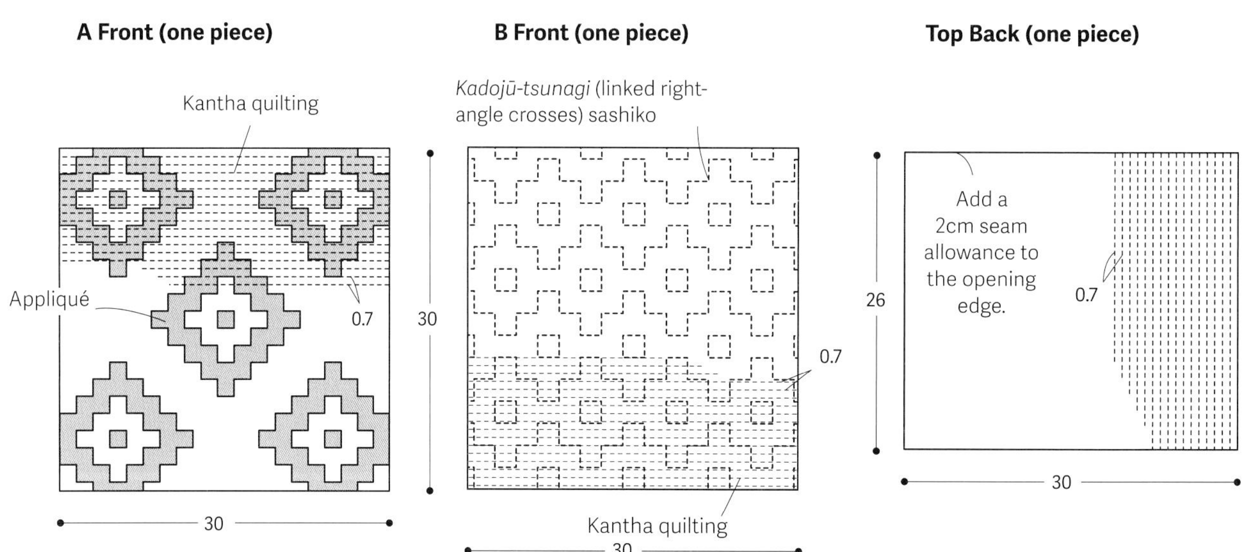

Bottom Back (one piece)

How to Make the Back

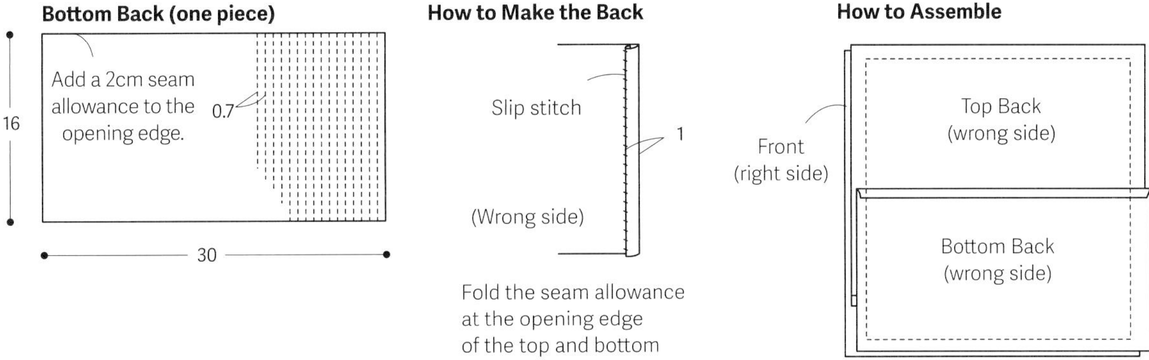

Fold the seam allowance at the opening edge of the top and bottom back pieces into a triple fold and slip stitch it closed.

How to Assemble

Place the front piece and both back pieces right sides together, and sew around the edges.

A Pattern
Photocopy at 100%

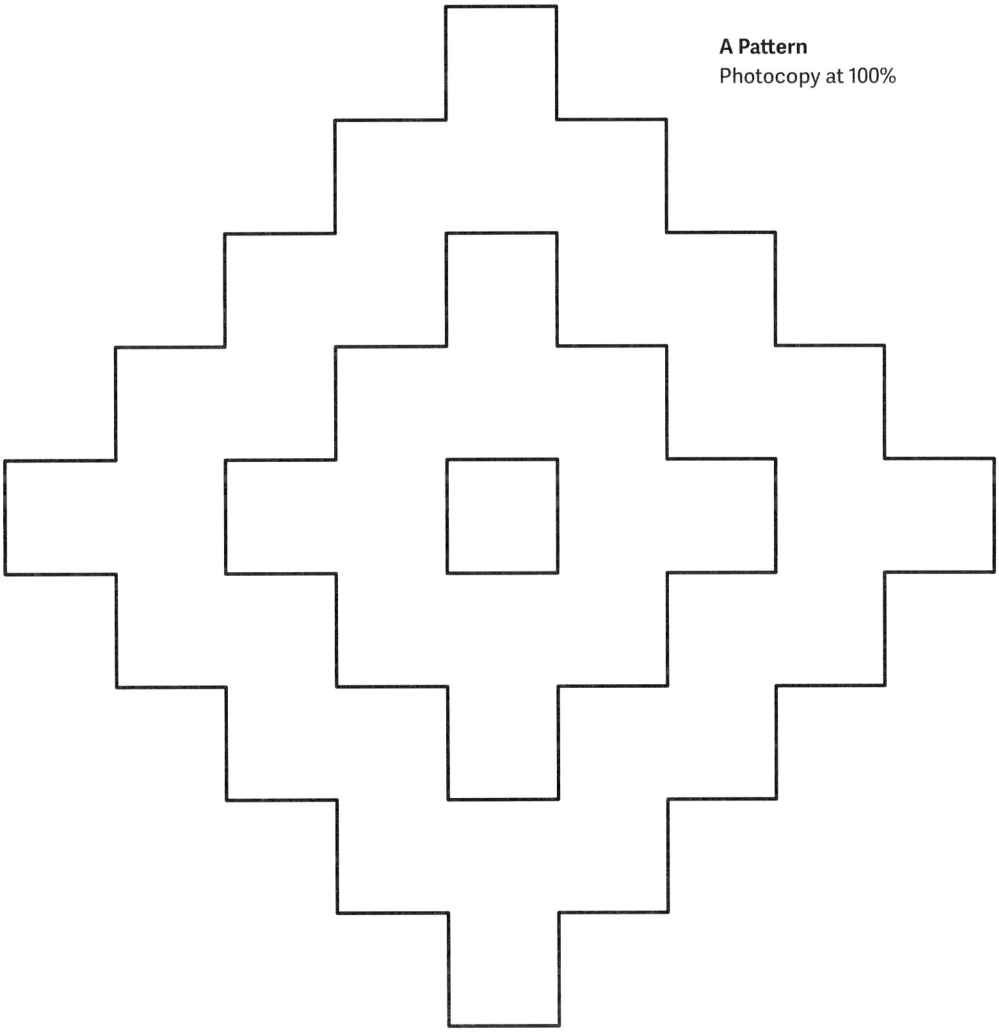

B Pattern
Photocopy at 100%

PAGE 20 → LARGE MULTIPURPOSE CLOTHS

Finished size:

64 × 100cm

Materials (for one cloth):

Outer fabric (two types): 110 × 75cm each
Inner fabric: 110 × 200cm
DARUMA Sashiko Thread (Thin) in color: 215 (Navy Blue)

Tip:

- For kantha, layer two to four pieces of inner fabric. Adjust the number and size of layers depending on the fabric.

Instructions:

1. Place the two outer pieces right sides together, layer the inner fabric below, and sew around the edges, leaving an opening for turning.
2. Turn right side out, slip stitch the opening closed, and do the kantha quilting.

Outer Layer (two pieces)

How to Assemble

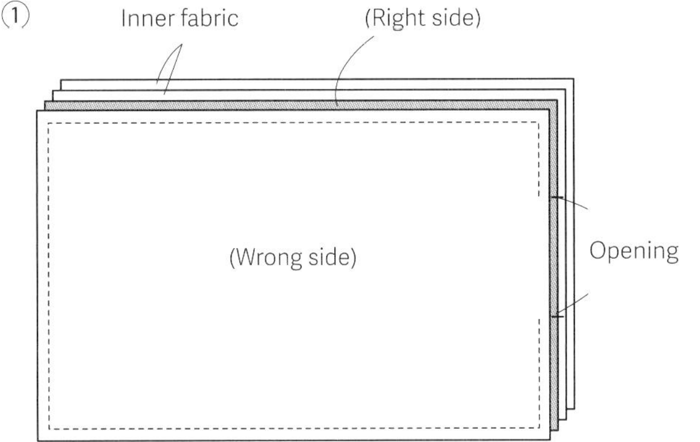

Place the two outer pieces right sides together, layer the inner fabric (same size) on one side (shown behind). Sew around the edges, leaving an opening for turning.

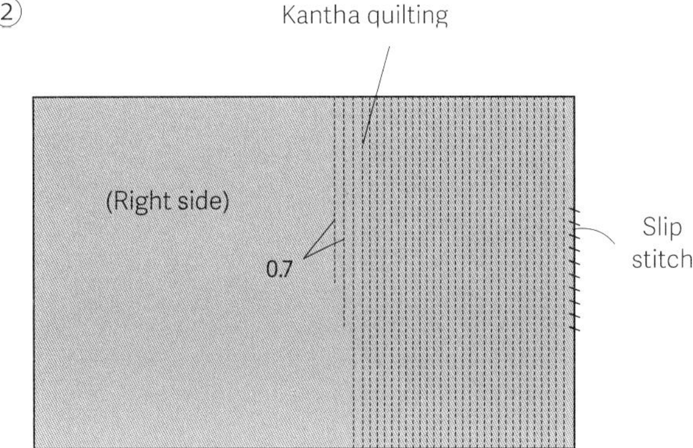

Turn the piece right side out, slip stitch the opening closed, and do the kantha quilting.

PAGE 22 → SIMPLE DRAWSTRING BAGS

Finished size:

22 × 24cm

Materials (for one bag):

Outer fabric and lining fabric: 30 × 50cm each
Inner fabric: 55 × 50cm
Cord: 0.5cm diameter, 320cm length
DARUMA Sashiko Thread (Thin) in colors: 202 (Ecru) (white, green, floral bag only), 219 (Black) (black bag only)

Tips:

- For fabrics with a directional print, cut the fabric into two pieces and join them at the bottom.
- For kantha, layer two to four pieces of inner fabric. Adjust the number and size of layers depending on the fabric.
- Use any cord you like.

Instructions:

1. Layer the outer fabric with the inner fabric and do the kantha quilting.
2. Place the outer and lining fabrics right sides together and sew along the top and bottom.
3. Fold so the seam allowances are on top of each other, keeping right sides together. Sew the sides, leaving openings for turning and threading the cords.
4. Turn it out, close the turning opening, and sew the channel for the cord.
5. Thread the cord through and tie it. Add tassels or other decorations if you like.

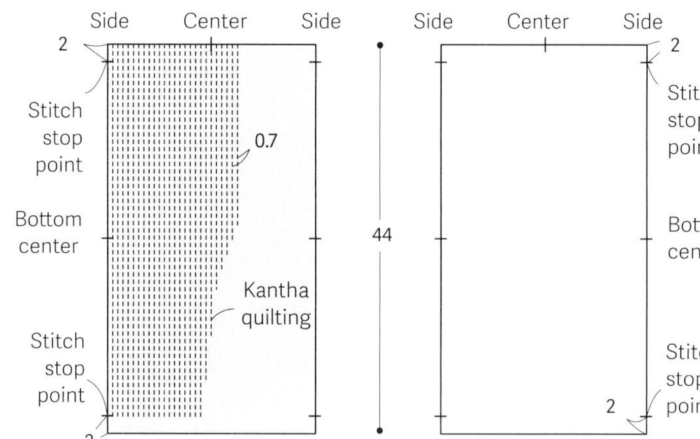

How to Assemble

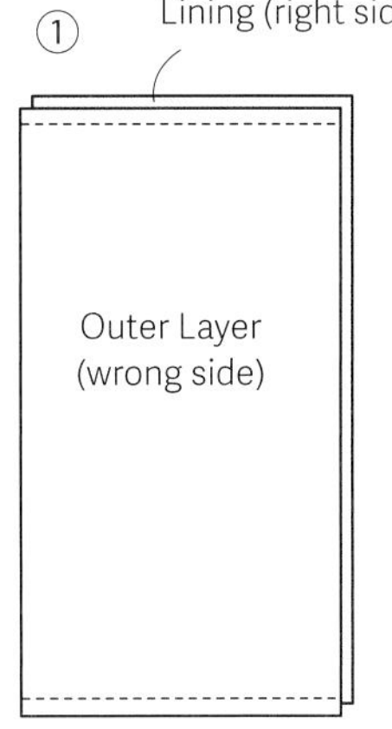

Place the outer piece and the lining right sides together and sew along the top and bottom.

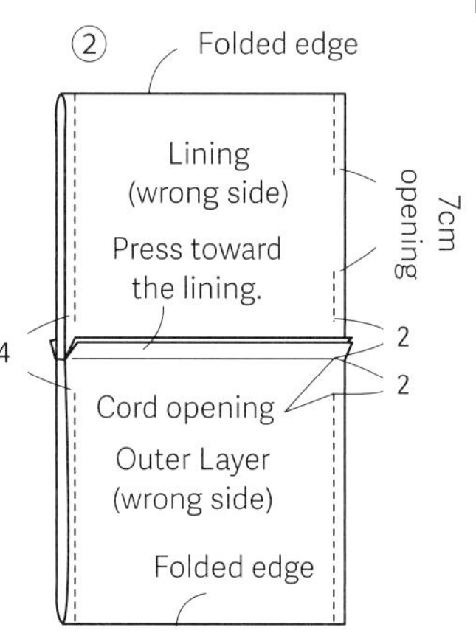

Fold so the bottom centers are now on top and bottom (keep right sides together). Sew the sides, leaving two openings for the cords and one for turning.

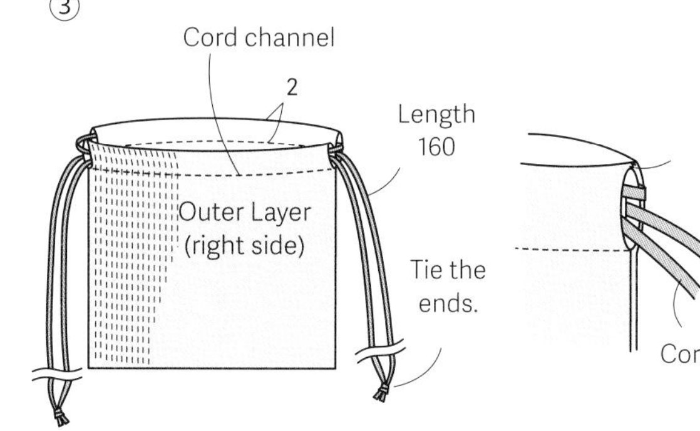

Turn it right side out, close the turning opening with ladder stitch, sew the cord channel, and thread the cord through.

PAGE 24 → MINI TOTE BAGS

Finished size:
27 × 25cm

Materials (for one bag):
Outer fabric: 65 × 35cm
Lining fabric: 30 × 60cm
Inner fabric: 60 × 100cm
Appliqué fabric scraps (for A only)
Handles: 3cm wide, 65cm length
DARUMA Home Thread (Fine) in color: 35 (Faded) (A only)
DARUMA Sashiko Thread (Thin) in color: 202 (Ecru) (B & C only)
Appliqué sashiko thread of your choice

Tips:
- Appliqué stitching can be done freely.
- For kantha, layer two to four pieces of inner fabric. Adjust the number and size of layers depending on the fabric.

Instructions:
1. For A, appliqué the front and back.
2. Layer the outer fabric (B & C) or front and back (A) with the inner fabric and do the kantha quilting.
3. With right sides together, sew the sides and bottom of the outer fabric.
4. Make the lining.
5. Fold the top edge of the outer piece (B & C) or front and back (A), and sew the handles in place.
6. Insert bag into the lining, slip stitch, and turn it out.

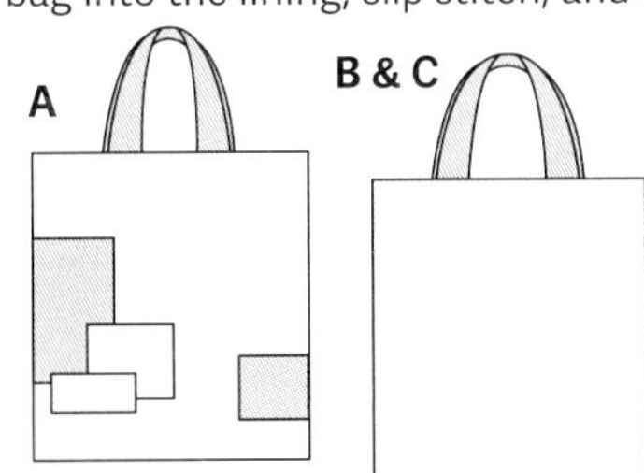

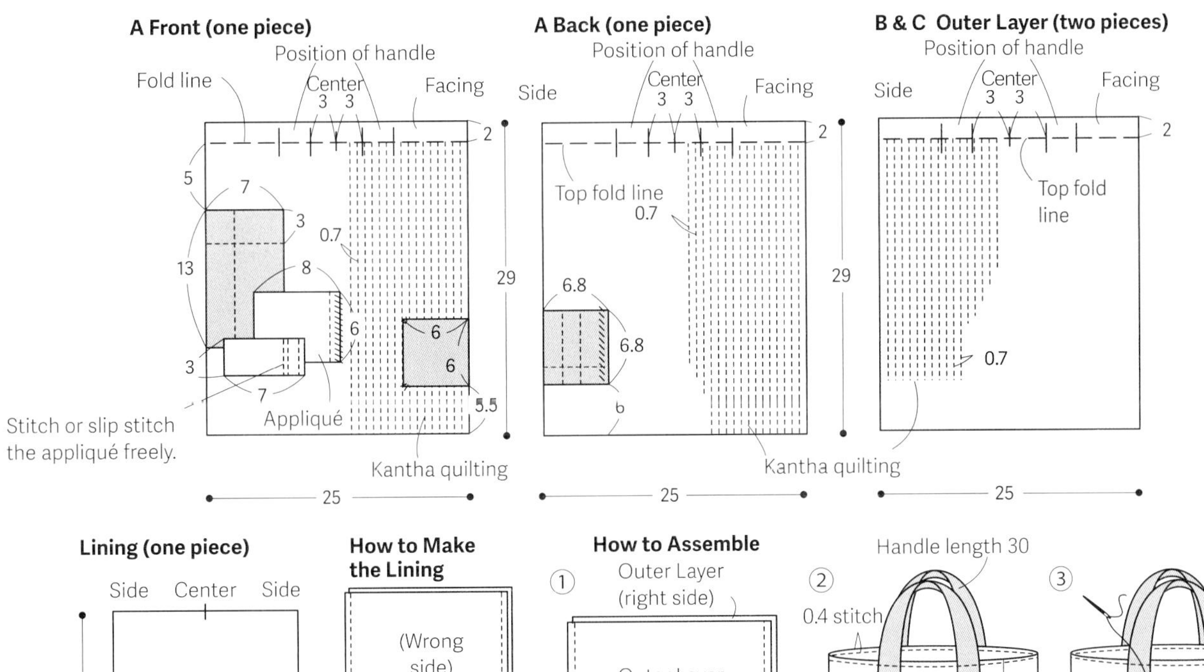

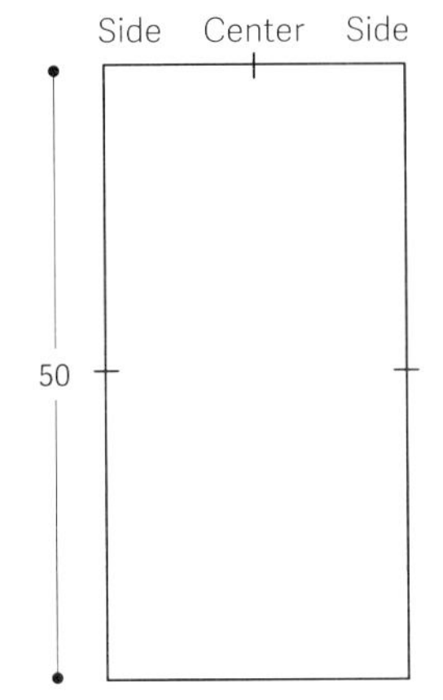

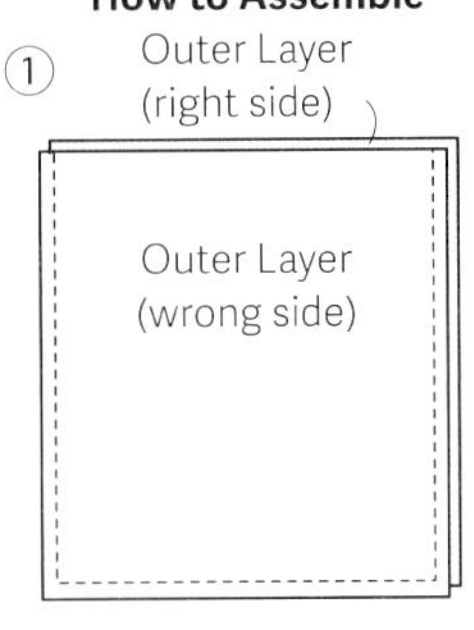

Fold in half with right sides together and sew both side edges.

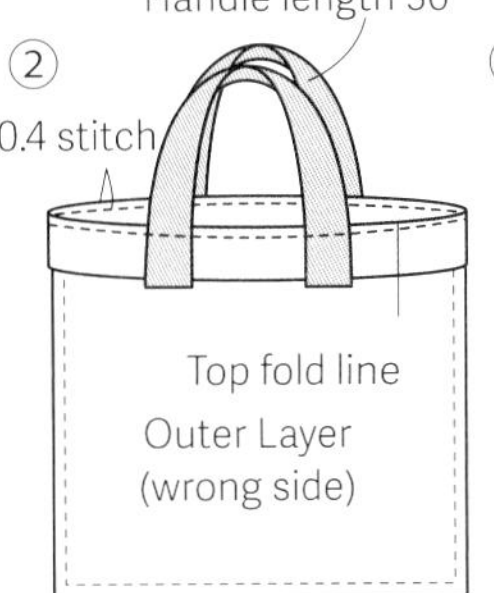

Place the two outer pieces right sides together and sew the three sides.

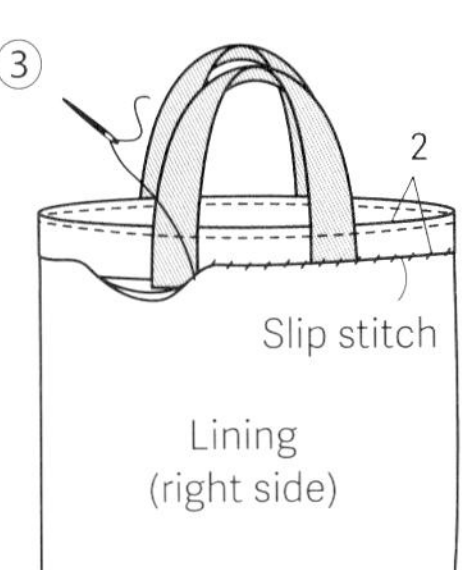

Fold back the top edge of the outer piece, layer the handles, and sew along the opening.

Fold in the seam allowance of the lining, align it with the outer piece with right sides out, and slip stitch it in place.

PAGE 26 → PLACE MAT WITH FLORAL EMBROIDERY

Finished size:
29 × 40.5cm

Materials:
Outer fabric and lining fabric: 45 × 35cm each
Inner fabric: 45 × 65cm
Binding: 4cm wide, 150cm length
COSMO Size 25 Embroidery Floss in colors: 536A (Green), 107 (Red)
DARUMA Home Thread (Fine) in color: Off-White

Tips:

- For kantha, layer two to four sheets of inner fabric. Adjust the number of layers and their size depending on the fabric.
- Use three strands of embroidery floss when stitching.

Instructions:

1. Layer the outer fabric, inner fabric, and lining fabric, then do the kantha quilting and embroidery.
2. Finish the edges with binding strips.

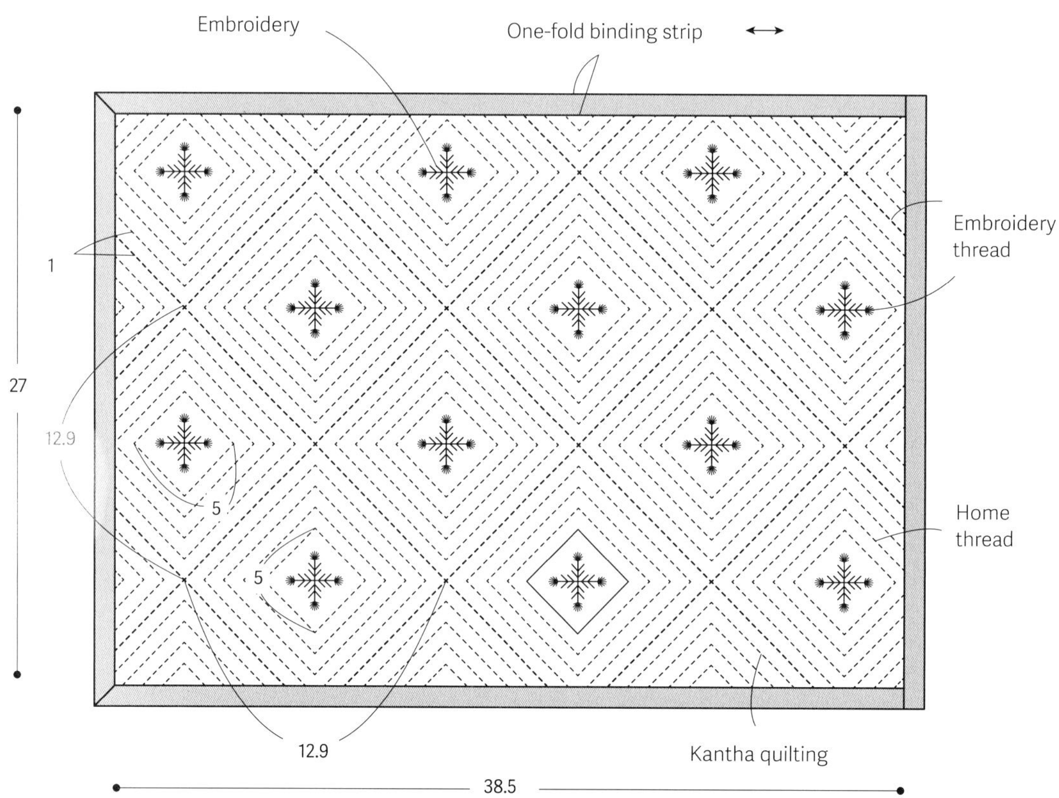

How to Stitch the Embroidery

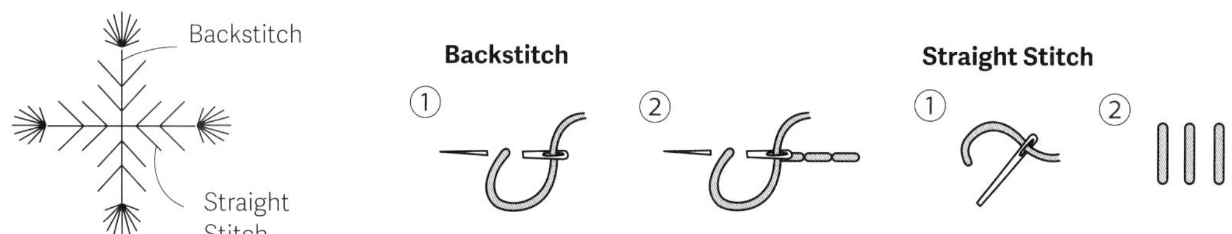

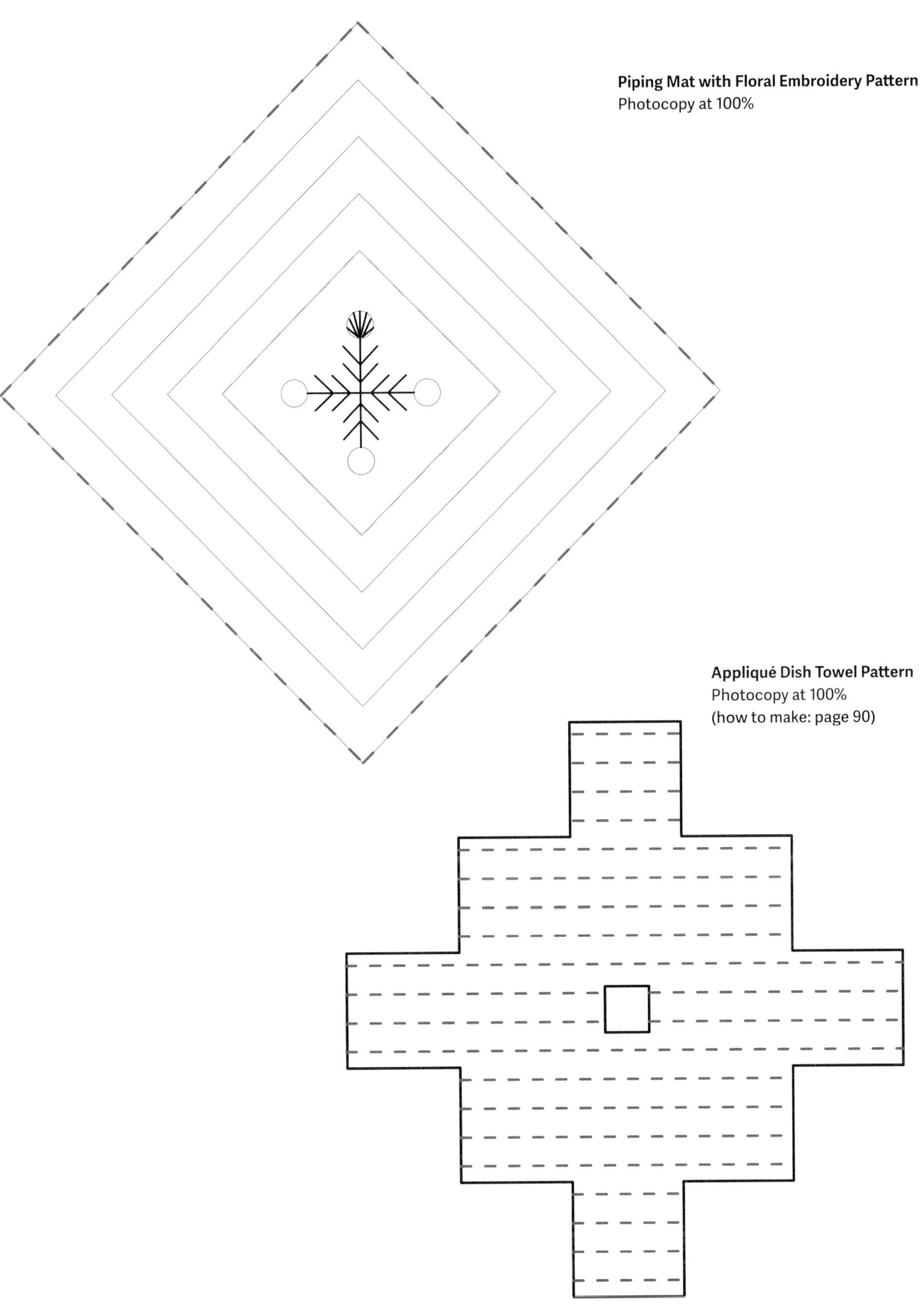

Piping Mat with Floral Embroidery Pattern
Photocopy at 100%

Appliqué Dish Towel Pattern
Photocopy at 100%
(how to make: page 90)

PAGE 28 → APPLIQUÉ DISH TOWEL

Finished size:
34.5 × 49cm

Materials:
Appliqué fabric: 40 × 25cm
Outer fabric and back fabric: 55 × 40cm each
Inner fabric: 55 × 80cm
DARUMA Home Thread (Fine) in color: 30 *(Kinari)*
DARUMA Sashiko Thread (Thin) in color: 229 (Grey)

Tips:

- For kantha, layer two sheets of inner fabric. Adjust the number of layers and their size depending on the fabric.
- For the appliqué pattern, refer to page 89.

Instructions:

1. Blind stitch the appliqué to the front fabric, layer it with the inner fabric, and do the kantha quilting.
2. With right sides together, sew the front and back together, leaving an opening for turning.
3. Turn right side out, slip stitch the opening closed, and add sashiko stitching around the edges.

Front (one piece)

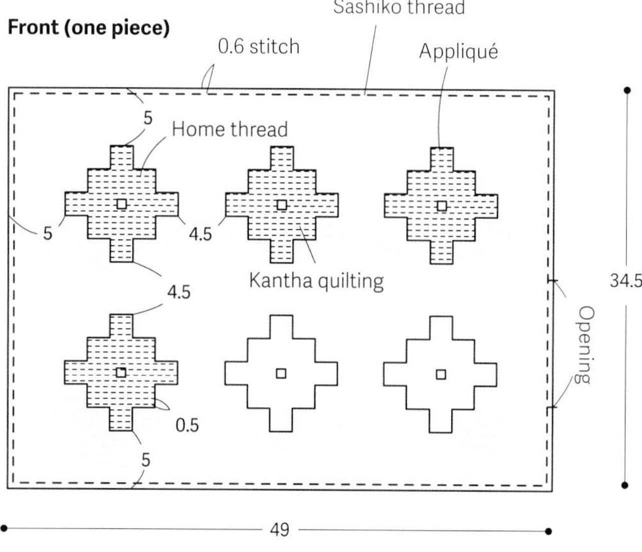

Back (one piece)

How to Assemble

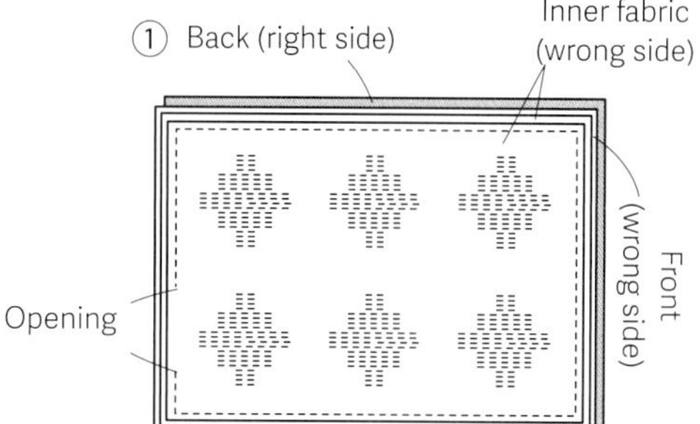

Place the front and back with right sides together, leaving an opening, and sew around the edges.

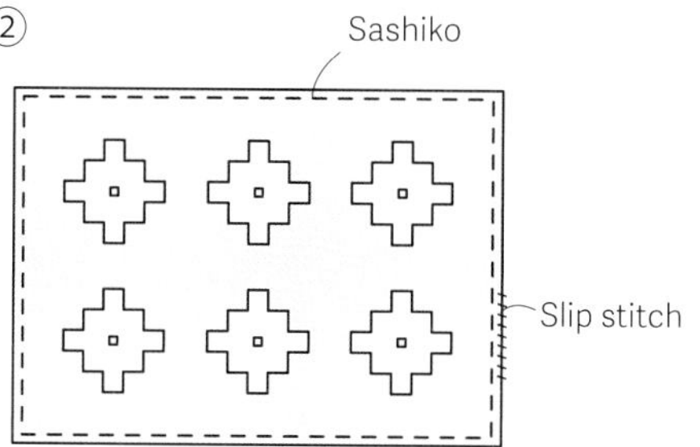

Turn right side out, slip stitch the opening closed, and add sashiko stitching around the edges.

PAGE 32 → BLACK ENVELOPE POUCHES

Finished size:

10.5 × 14cm

Materials (for one pouch):

Outer fabric (includes lining): 50 × 25cm

DARUMA Sashiko Thread (Thin) in color: 202 (Ecru)

Tip:

- For stitching methods, refer to pages 40–41 and 93.

Instructions:

1. Combine the outer fabric and lining fabric with right sides together, leaving an opening for turning, and sew around the edges.
2. Turn right side out and slip stitch the opening closed.
3. Do the sashiko stitching.
4. Bring the three corners together at the center and close with a ladder stitch.

A

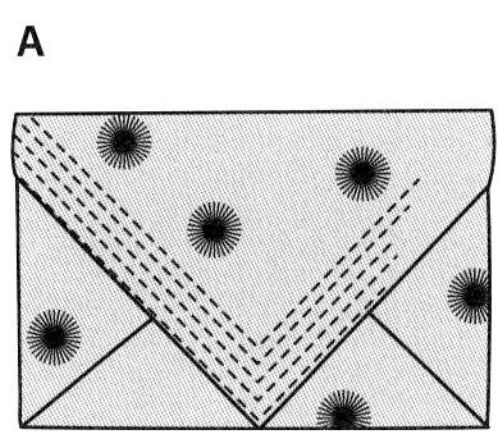

B

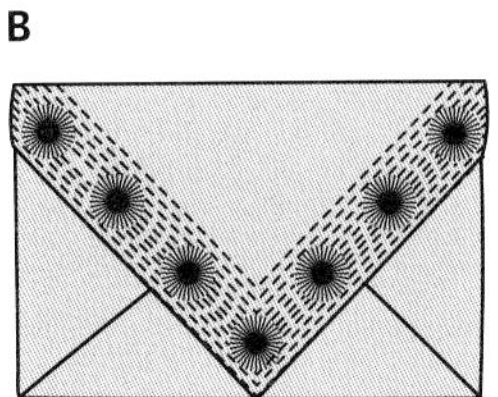

A Outer Layer (one piece)

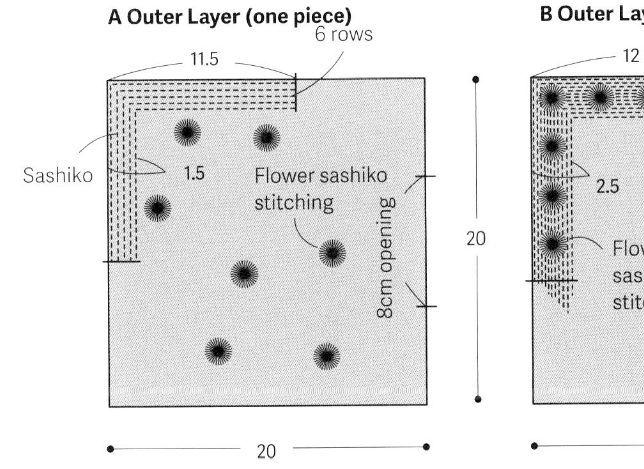

B Outer Layer (one piece)

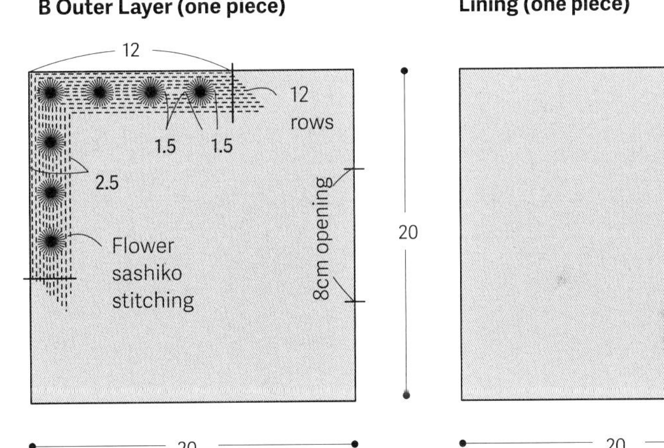

*Do the sashiko stitching after sewing the lining fabric in place.

Lining (one piece)

How to Assemble

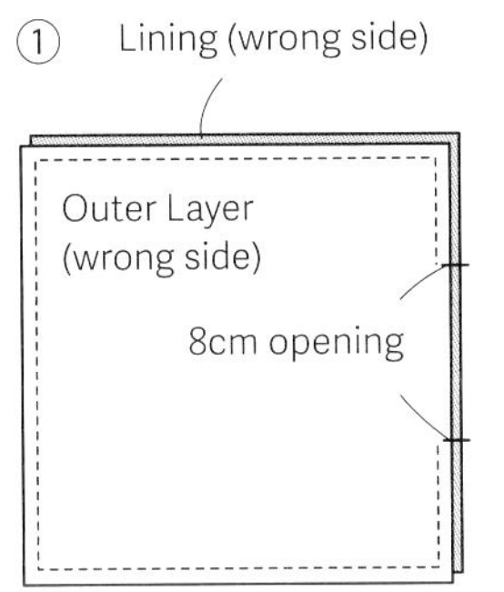

Place the pieces right sides together, leave an opening for turning, and sew around the edges.

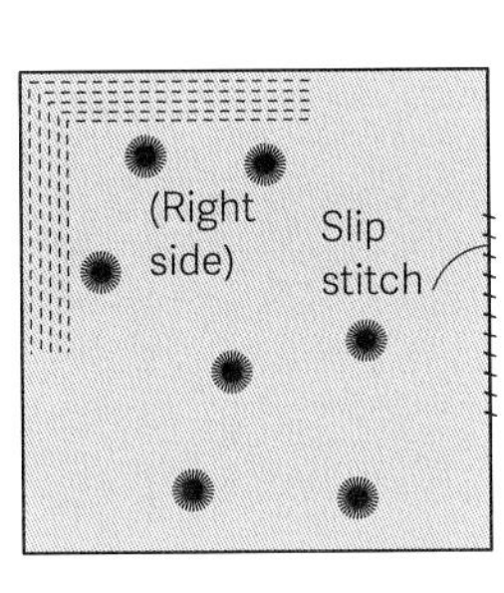

Turn it right side out, slip stitch the opening closed, and do the sashiko stitching.

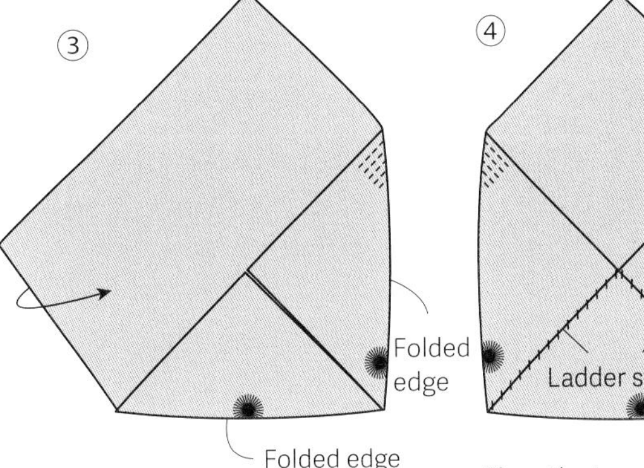

Bring the three corners together at the center.

Close the two sides using a ladder stitch.

PAGE 31 → NATURAL PINCUSHIONS

Finished size:
7 × 7cm

Materials (for one pincushion):
Outer fabric: 20 × 10cm
Craft stuffing, as needed
DARUMA Sashiko Thread (Thin) in color: 202 (Ecru)

Tip:

- For stitching methods, also refer to pages 40–41.

Instructions:

1. Do the sashiko stitching on the front.
2. Place the front and back pieces right sides together, and sew around the edges, leaving an opening.
3. Turn it right side out, stuff, and slip stitch the opening closed.

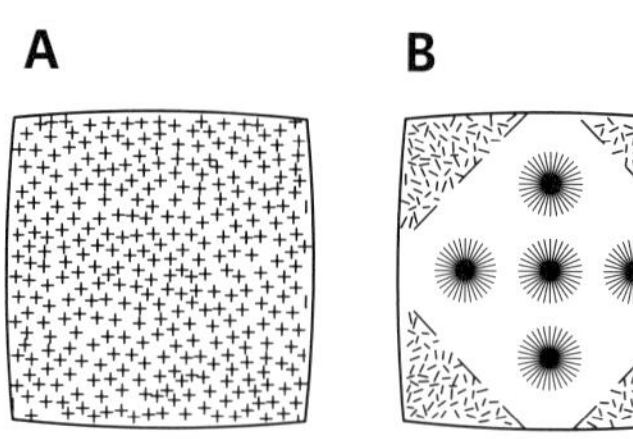

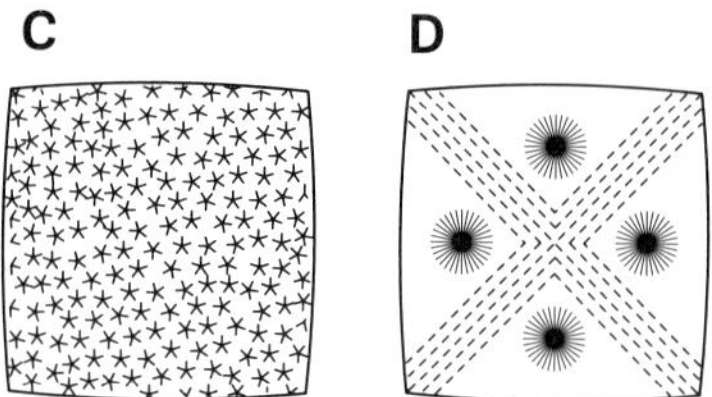

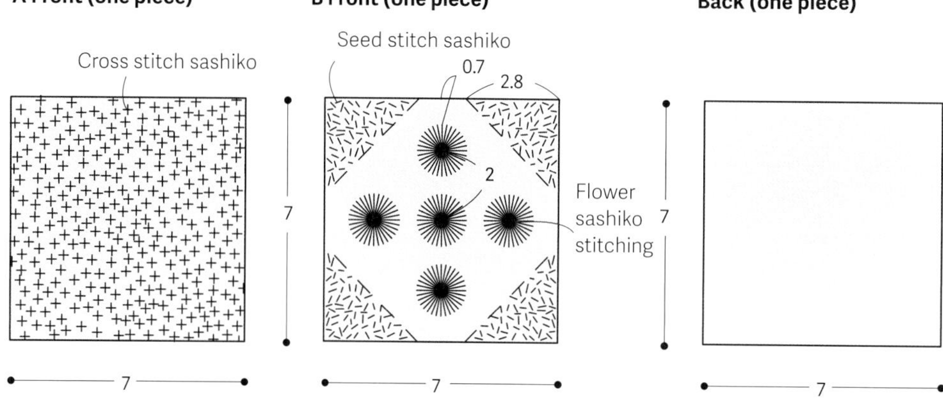

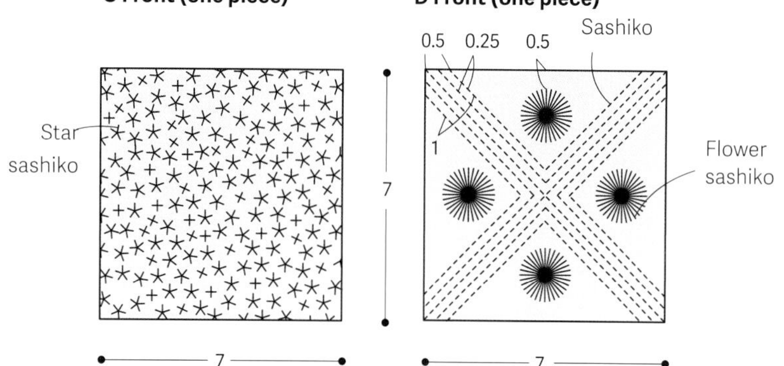

How to Assemble

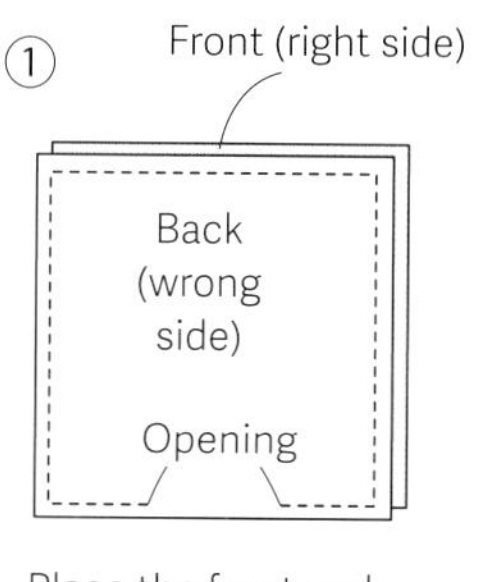

Place the front and back pieces with right sides together, leave an opening for turning, and sew around the edges.

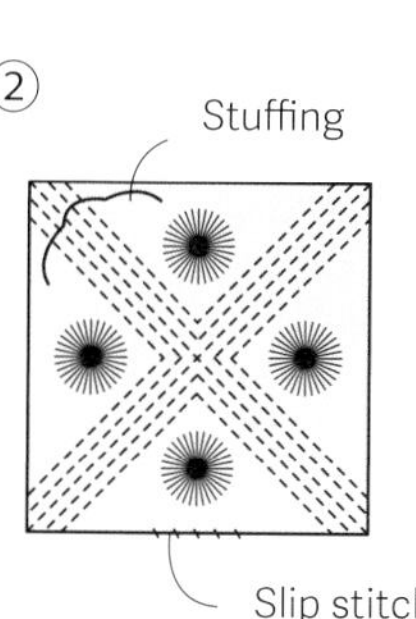

Turn it right side out, stuff, and slip stitch the opening closed.

B Pattern
Photocopy at 100%

D Pattern
Photocopy at 100%

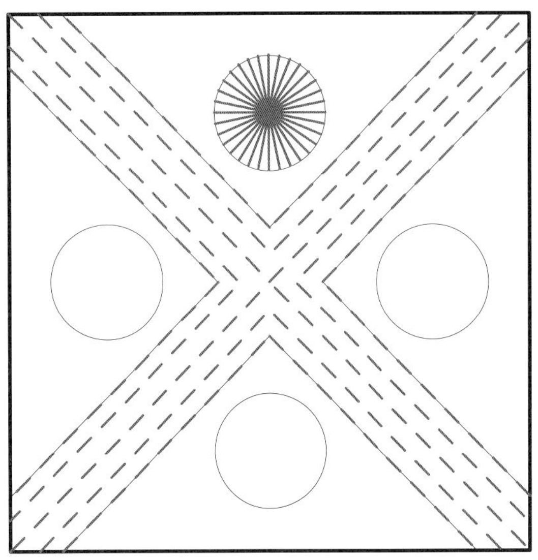

How to Stitch the Sashiko

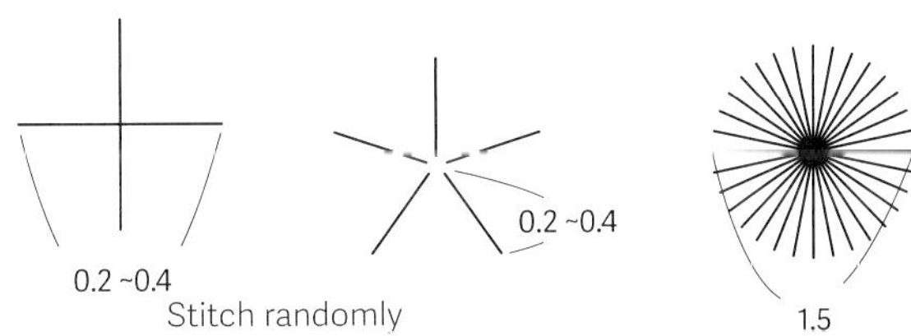

PAGE 34 → OVAL AND SQUARE CUFF BRACELETS

Finished size:
17 × 4cm

Materials (for one bracelet):
Outer fabric: 5 × 20cm
Lining fabric: 10 × 20cm
Closure fabric: 5 × 5cm
Twill tape: 3cm wide, 20cm length
Twill tape: 3.8cm wide, 20cm length
Waxed cord: 0.3cm diameter, 10cm length
Craft stuffing, as needed
DARUMA Sashiko Thread (Thin) in color: 202 (Ecru)

Tip:
- For stitching methods, refer to pages 40–41.

Instructions:
1. Do sashiko stitching on the outer fabric.
2. Layer the twill tape over the outer fabric, fold both ends in to wrap the edges.
3. Layer the twill tape over the lining fabric and wrap the edges.
4. Place the outer fabric on the lining, wrong sides together, and slip stitch it in place.
5. Fold in the edge of the lining fabric, cut the cord in half, thread one piece through each side, and slip stitch it to the outer fabric.
6. Create and attach a ball closure to the end of the cord.

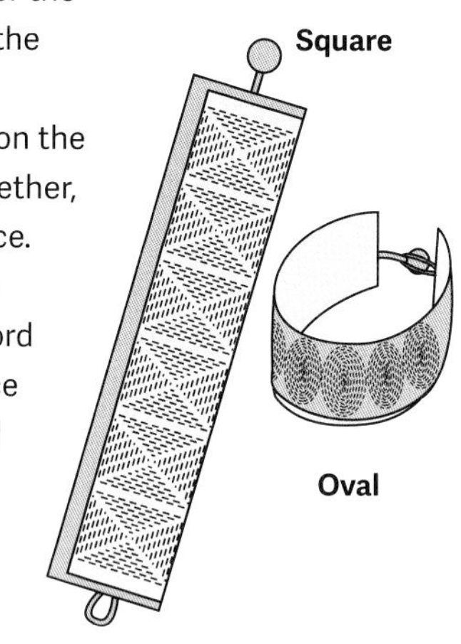

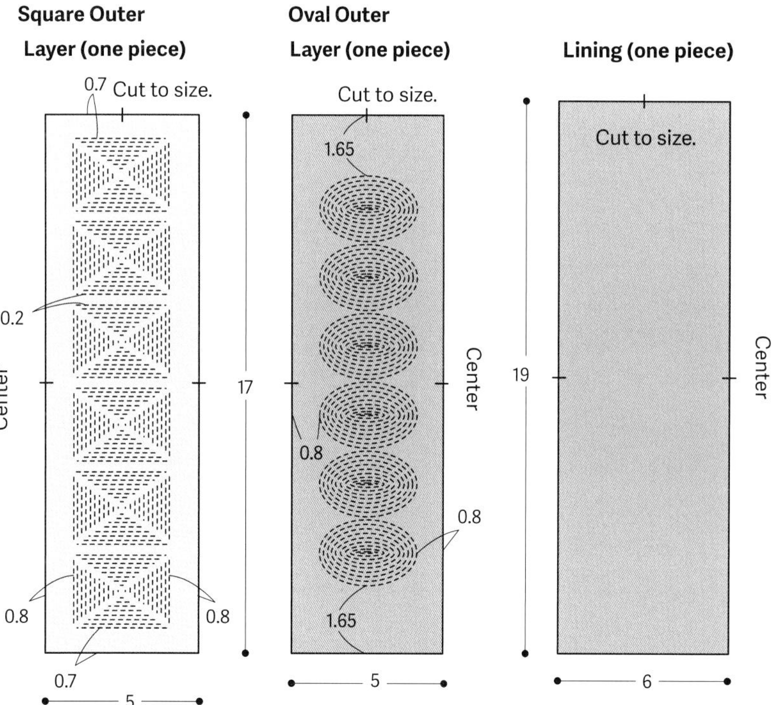

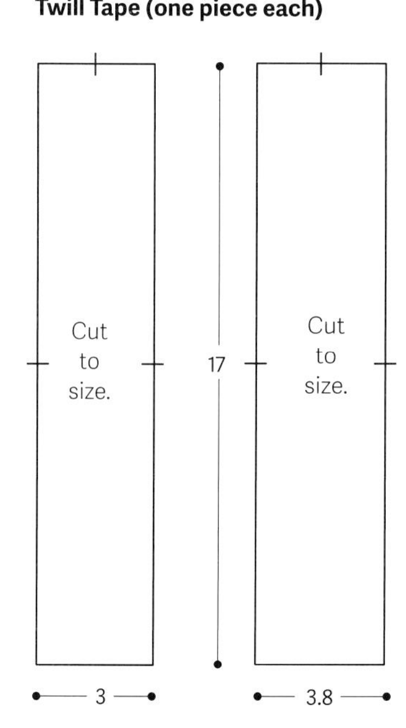

Closure (one piece)

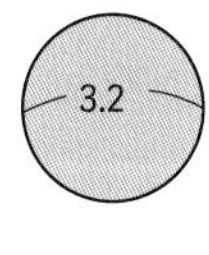

Cut to size.

How to Make the Ball Closure

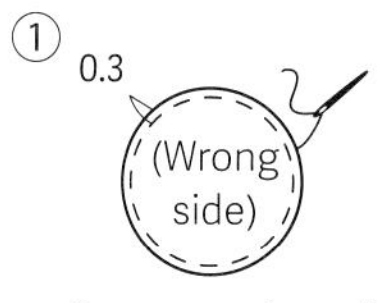

Sew a running stitch around the edge.

Stuff and while tucking in the seam allowance, pull the running stitch tight.

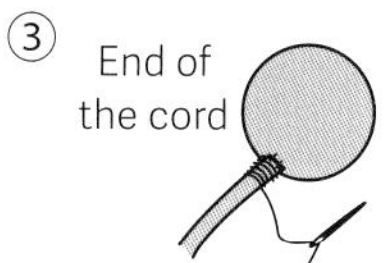

Insert the end of the cord and oversew it, then continue wrapping the thread around the cord.

How to Assemble

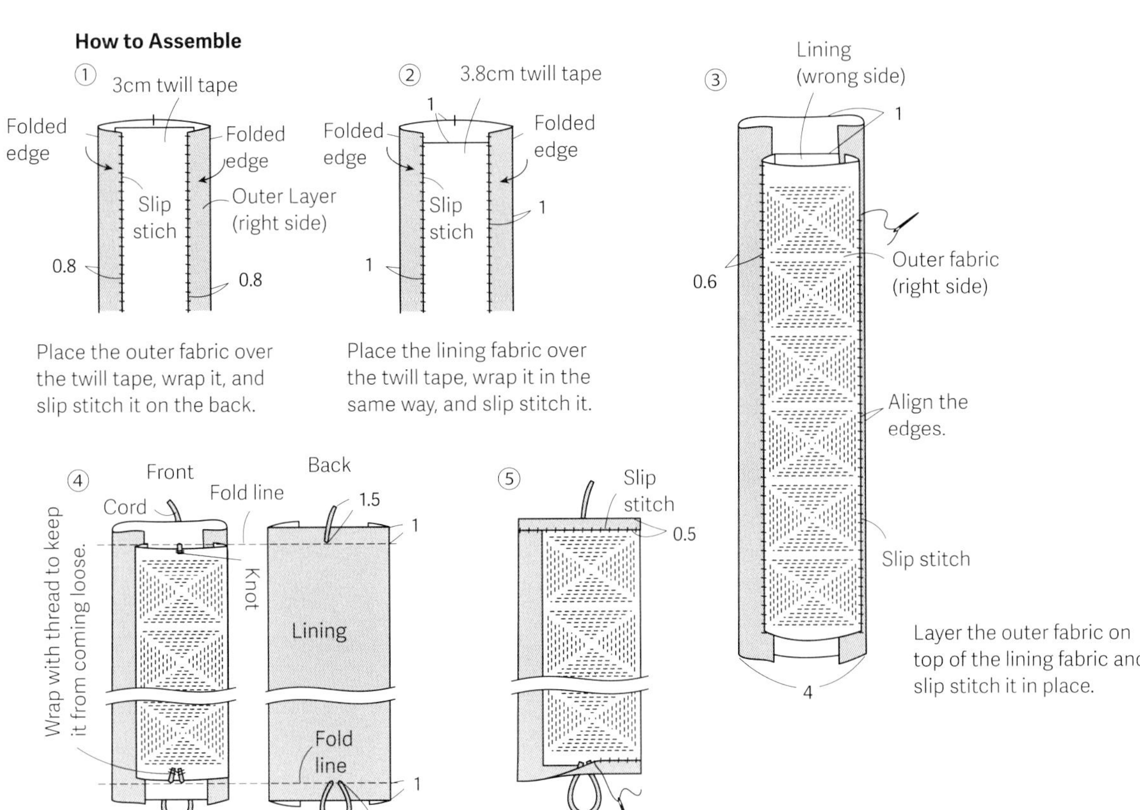

Photocopy at 100%

PAGE 36 → DIAGONAL GRID NEEDLE BOOKS

Finished size:

11.5 × 9cm

Materials (for one book):

Outer fabric (includes pocket): 35 × 15cm
Lining fabric and batting: 25 × 15cm each
Felt: 10 × 10cm
DARUMA Sashiko Thread (Thin) in color: 202 (Ecru)

Tip:

- For stitching methods, refer to pages 40–41.

Instructions:

1. Do the sashiko stitching on the outer fabric.
2. Sew the felt needle pad onto the lining fabric, then attach the pocket temporarily.
3. Place the outer fabric and lining fabric right sides together, layer the batting below, and sew around the edges, leaving an opening for turning.
4. Turn it right side out and slip stitch the opening closed.

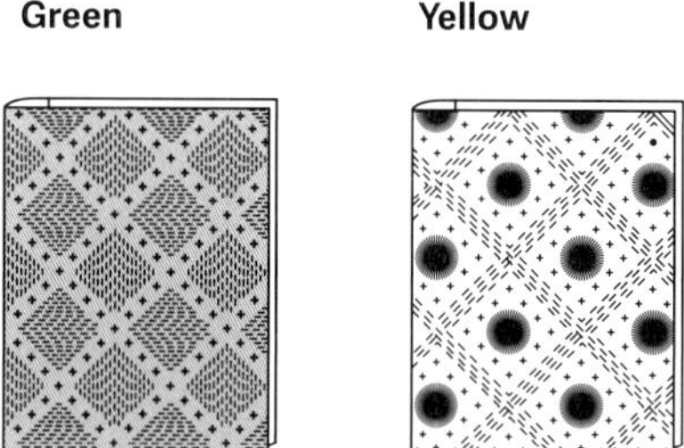

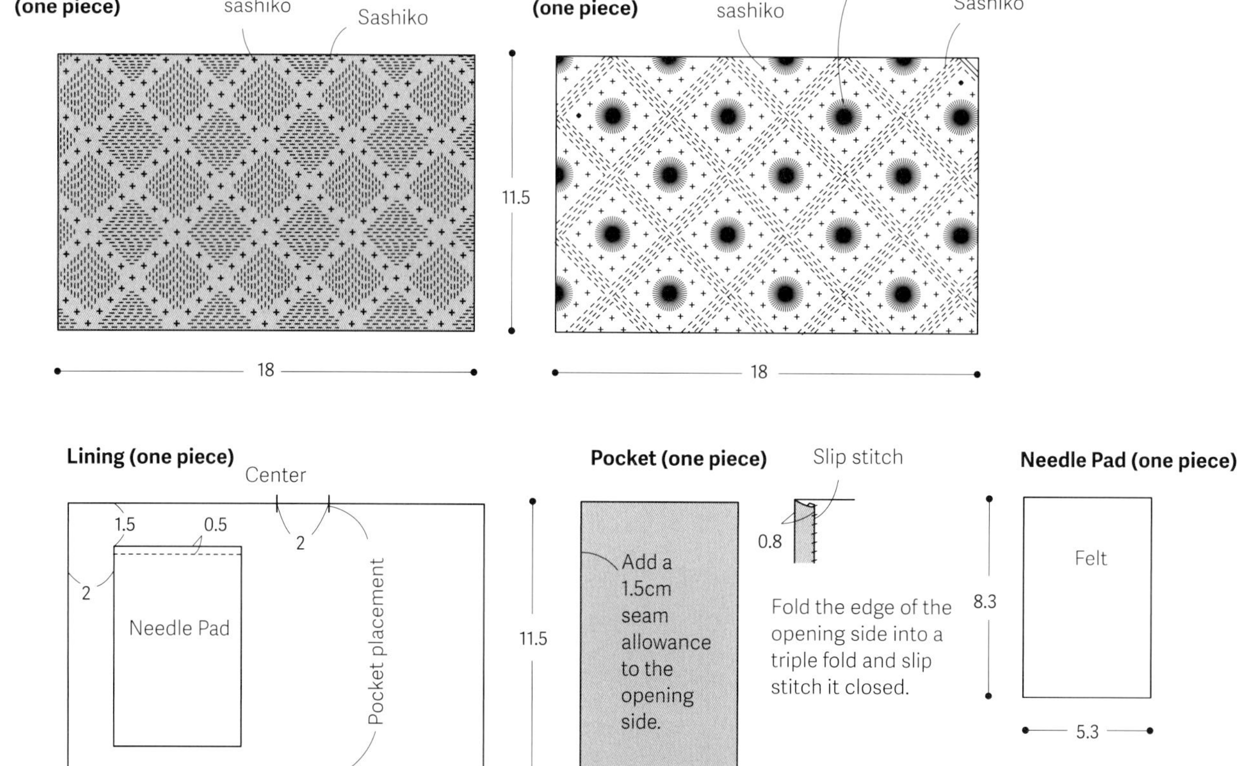

How to Assemble

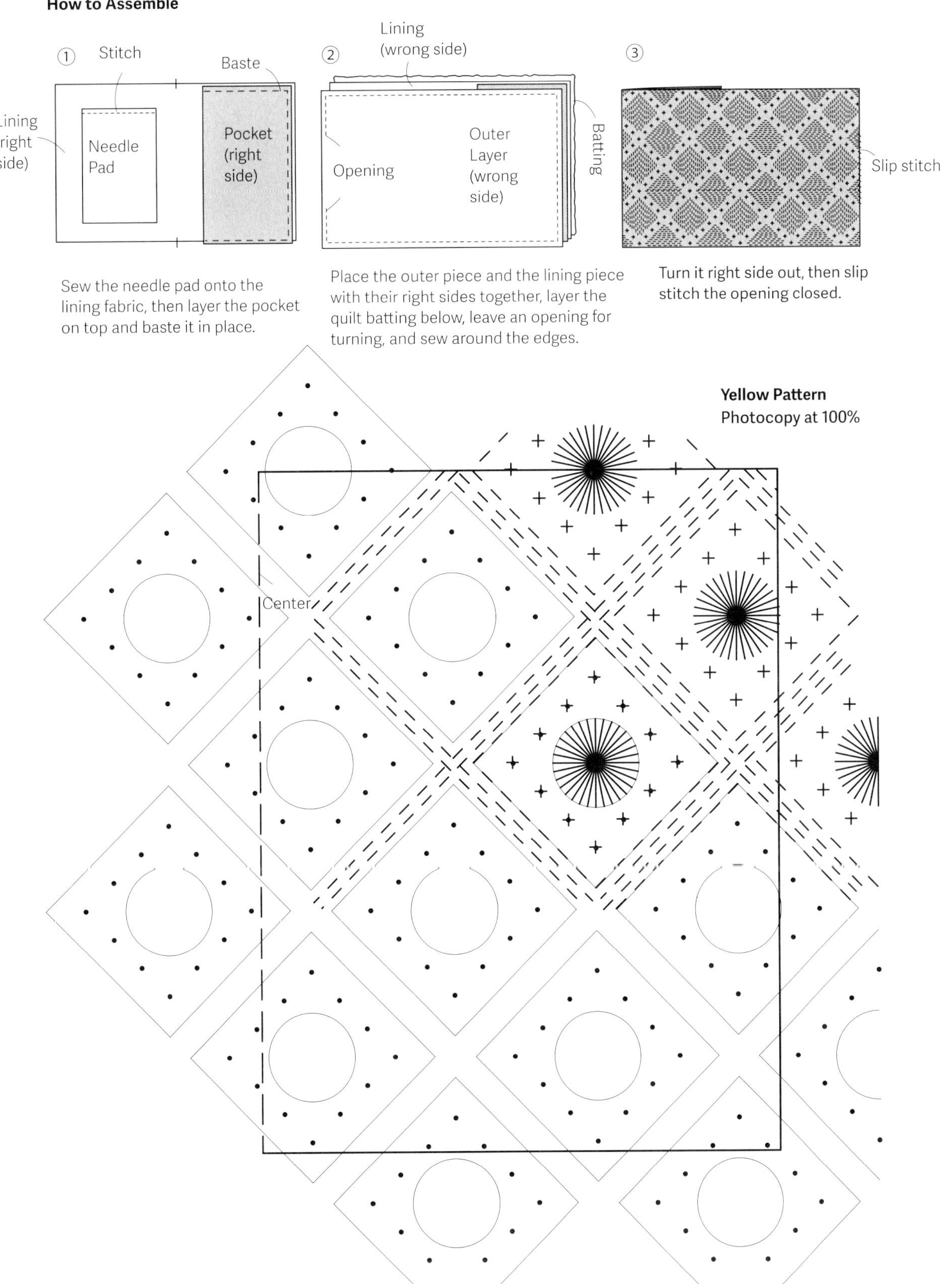

① Sew the needle pad onto the lining fabric, then layer the pocket on top and baste it in place.

② Place the outer piece and the lining piece with their right sides together, layer the quilt batting below, leave an opening for turning, and sew around the edges.

③ Turn it right side out, then slip stitch the opening closed.

Yellow Pattern
Photocopy at 100%

Green Pattern
Photocopy at 100%

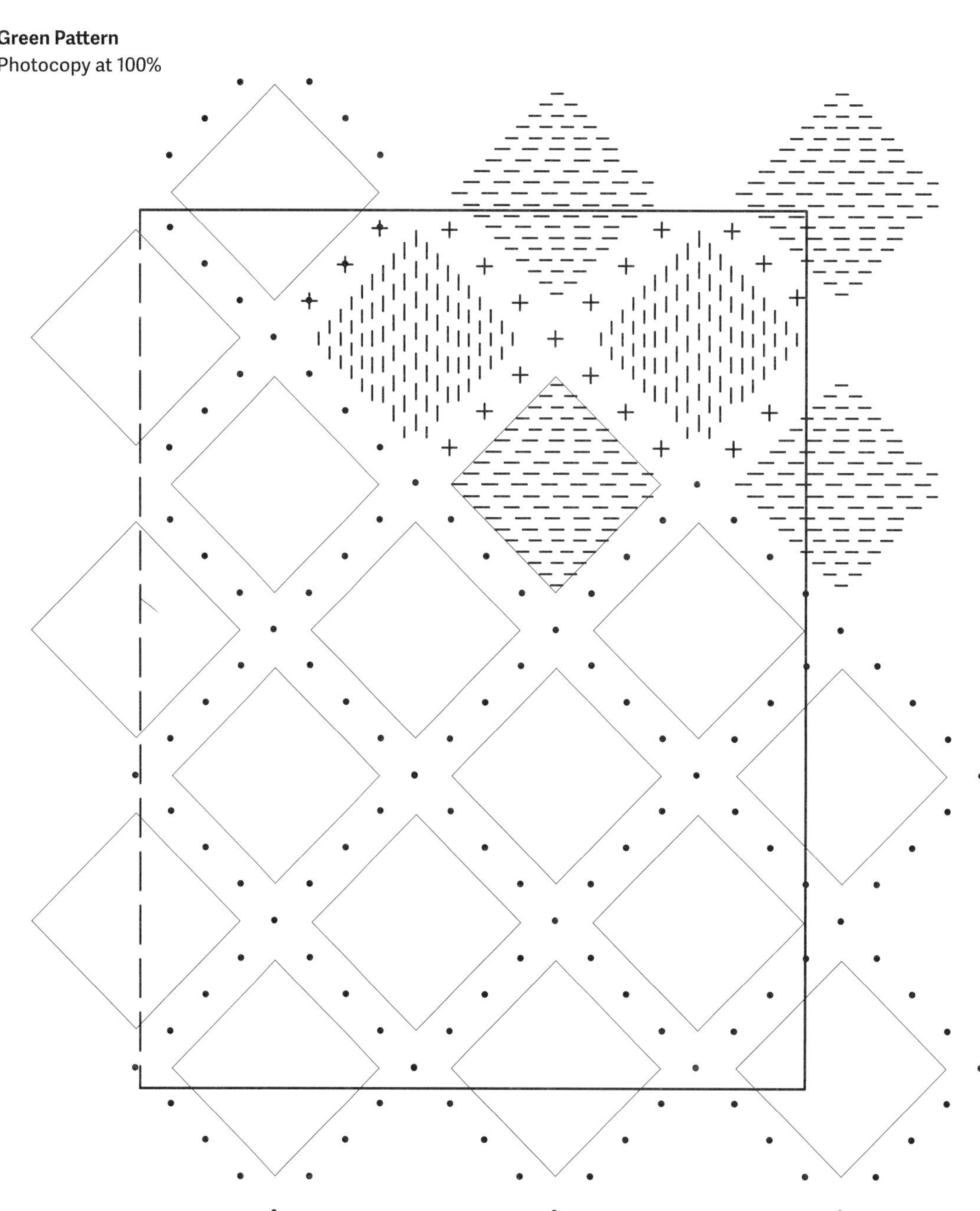

PAGE 38 → STRIPED MAT

Finished size:
27.5 × 40cm

Materials:
Outer fabric: 40 × 35cm
DARUMA Sashiko Thread (Thick) in color: 202 (Ecru)

Tips:
- Only trace the outline of the stripes, then sashiko stitch freely and randomly within them.
- For stitching methods, refer to pages 40–41.

Instructions:
1. Do sashiko stitching on the outer fabric.
2. Fold the top and bottom edges into a triple fold, and slip stitch them in place.

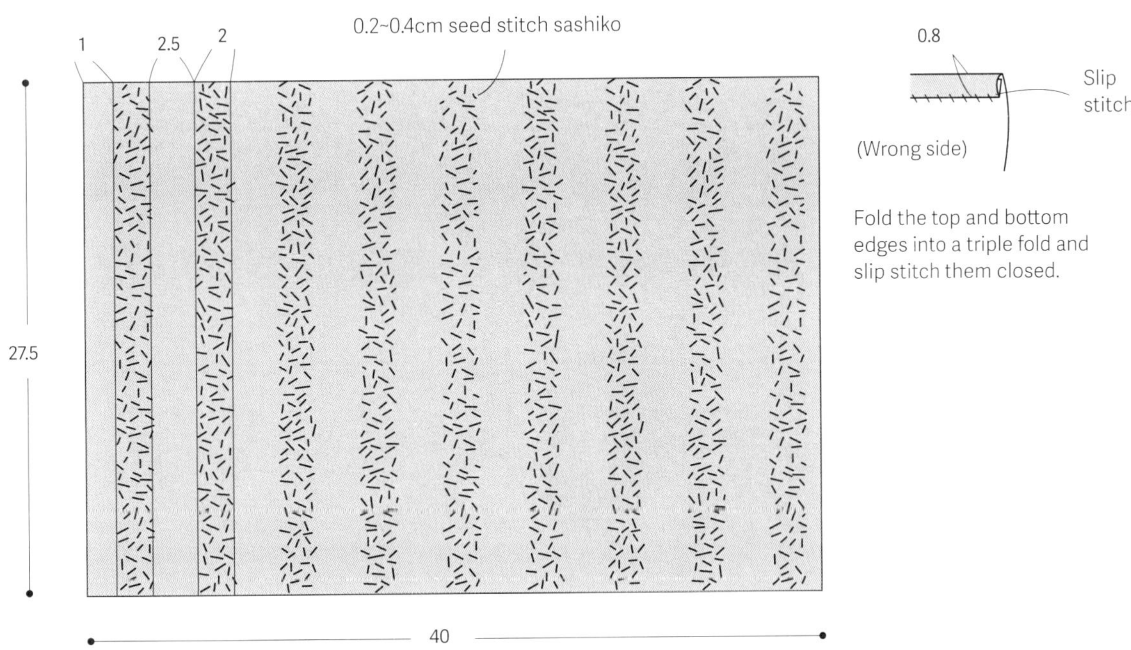

*For the width, use the full fabric width as is. Add a 1.5cm seam allowance to both the top and bottom.

PAGE 43 → STAGGERED-STITCH *FUROSHIKI*

Finished size:

53 × 53cm

Materials:

Outer fabric: 115 × 60cm

DARUMA Sashiko Thread (Thick) in colors: 202 (Ecru), 215 (Navy Blue)

Tips:

- For stitching methods, refer to page 57.
- Use two strands of sashiko thread.

Instructions:

1. Place the two outer fabric pieces right sides together and sew around the edges, leaving an opening for turning.
2. Turn right side out, slip stitch the opening closed, and do the sashiko stitching.

Outer Layer (two pieces)

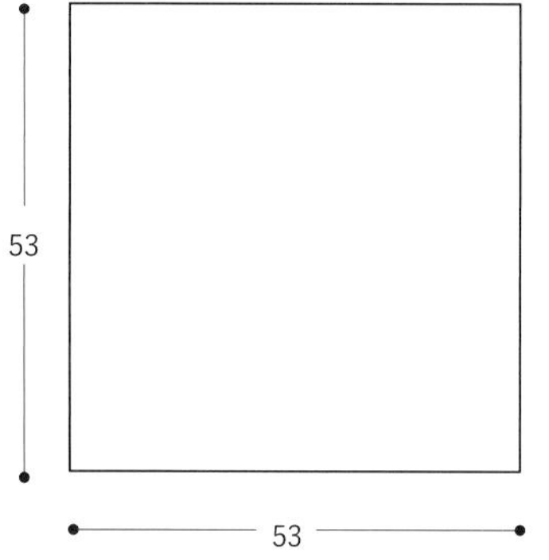

How to Assemble

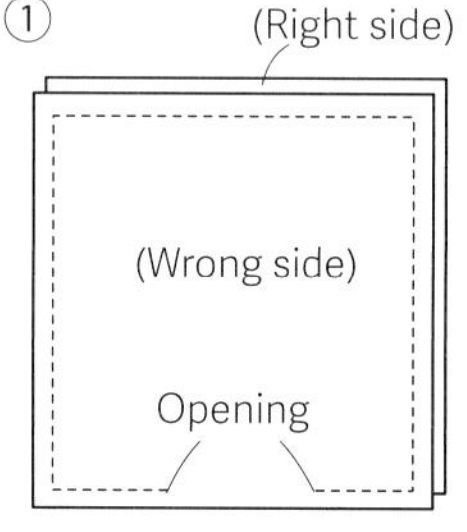

Place the pieces right sides together, leaving an opening for turning, and sew around the edges.

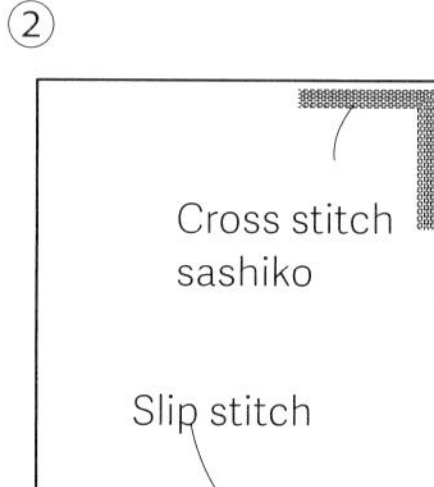

Turn it right side out, slip stitch the opening closed, and work the staggered sashiko stitching.

How to Stitch the Sashiko

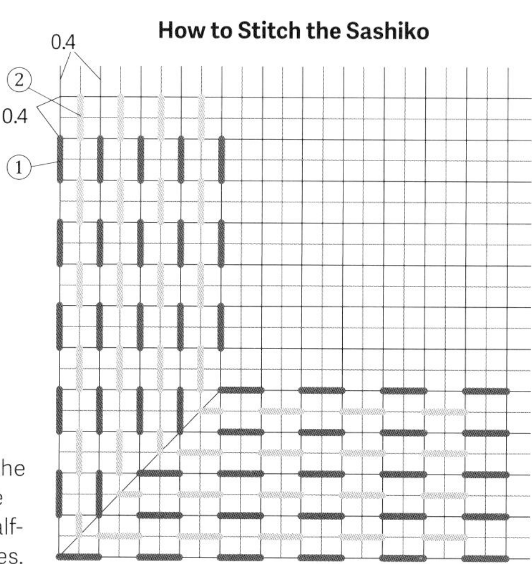

At the points where the stitches intersect the diagonal lines, use half-length (0.2cm) stitches.

Draw a 0.4cm grid and mark the diagonals. First, do sashiko stitching along line ① for five rows. Then, stitch line ② for four rows so that it alternates with the previous rows.

PAGE 44 → LATTICE PLACE MAT

Finished size:
28 × 40.5cm

Materials:
Outer fabric: 40.5 × 30cm
DARUMA Sashiko Thread (Thick) in color: 219 (Black)

Tip:

- Draw guidelines directly on the fabric before stitching.

Instructions:

1. Do sashiko stitching on the outer fabric.
2. Fold the top and bottom edges into a triple fold and slip stitch them closed.

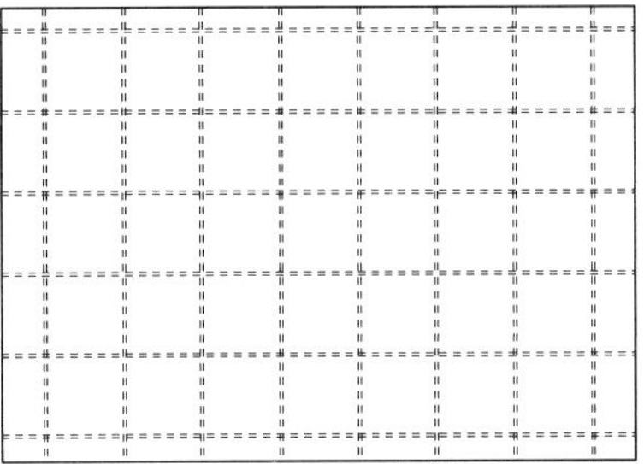

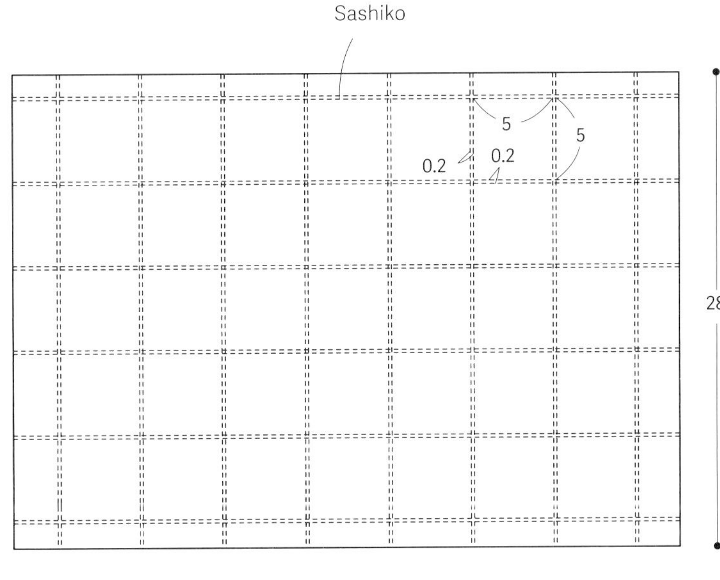

*For the width, use the full fabric width as is. Add a 1.5cm seam allowance to both the top and bottom.

How to Stitch the Sashiko

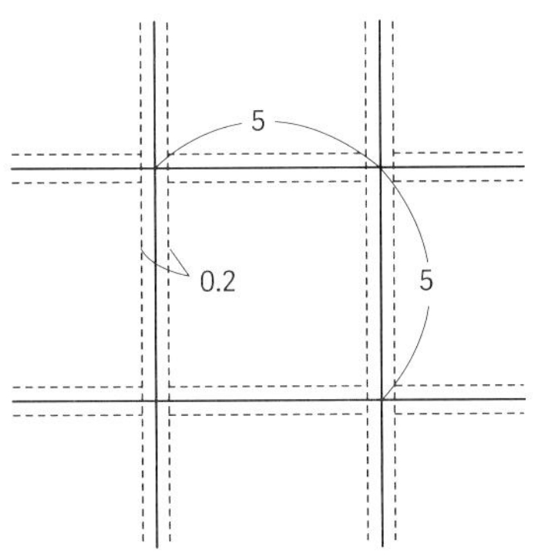

Stitch two lines evenly on either side of the guideline.

How to Assemble

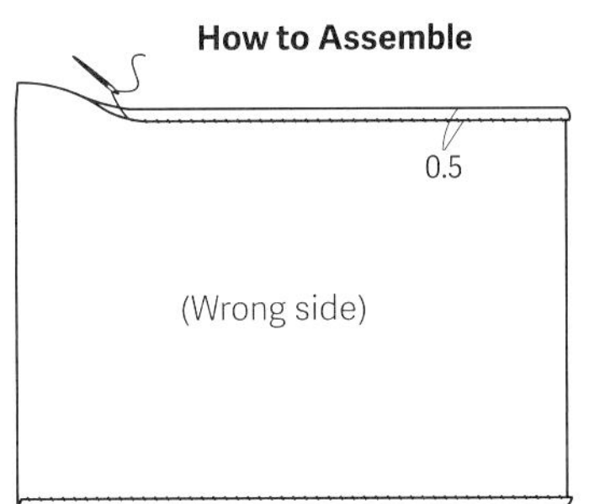

PAGE 46 → *WARIKIKU* ENVELOPE POUCH

Finished size:
10.5 × 14cm

Materials (for one pouch):
Outer fabric (includes lining): 50 × 25cm
DARUMA Sashiko Thread (Thin) in colors: 202 (Ecru), 219 (Black)

Tip:
- For stitching methods, refer to pages 56–57.

Instructions:
1. Place the outer fabric and lining with right sides together, leaving an opening for turning, and sew around the edges.
2. Turn right side out and slip stitch the opening closed.
3. Do the sashiko stitching.
4. Bring the three corners together in the center and stitch closed using ladder stitch.

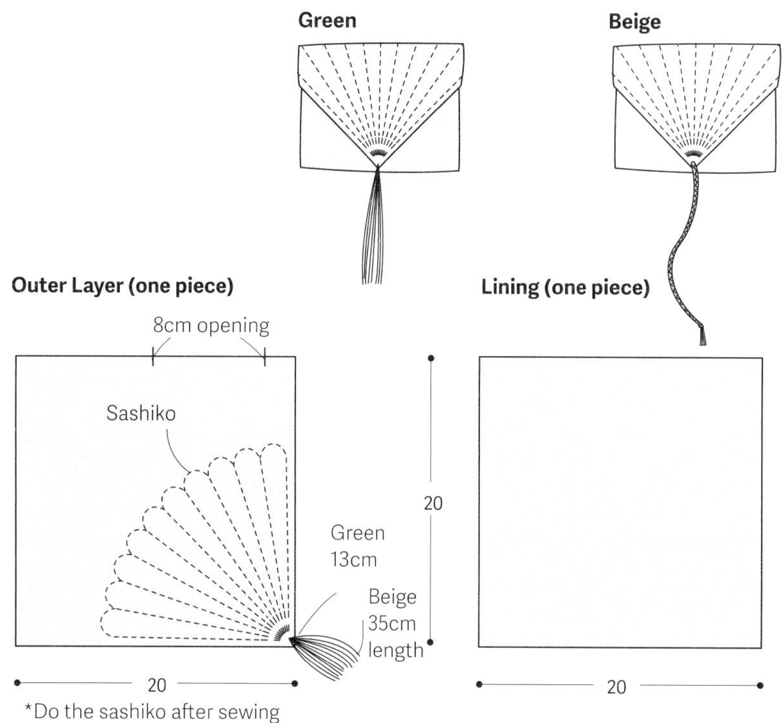

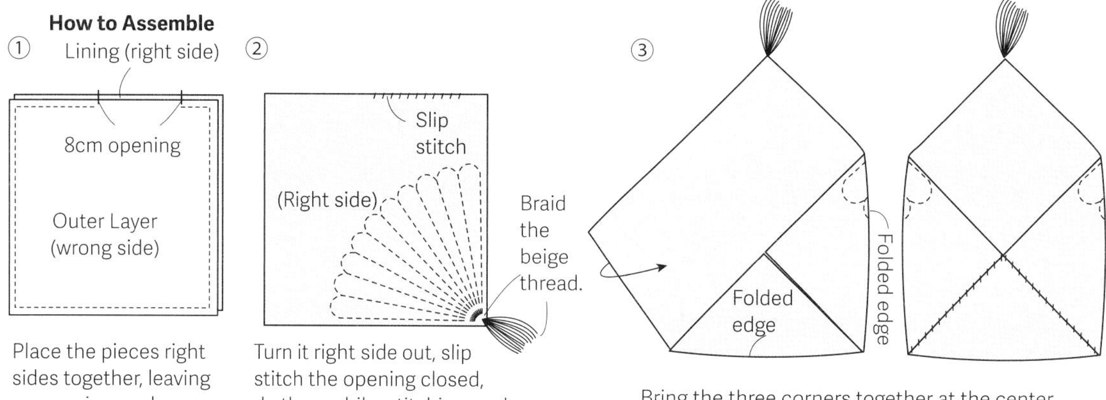

① Place the pieces right sides together, leaving an opening, and sew around the edges.

② Turn it right side out, slip stitch the opening closed, do the sashiko stitching, and bring the thread out from the corner, leaving it hanging.

③ Bring the three corners together at the center and use ladder stitch to close two sides.

How to Stitch the Sashiko

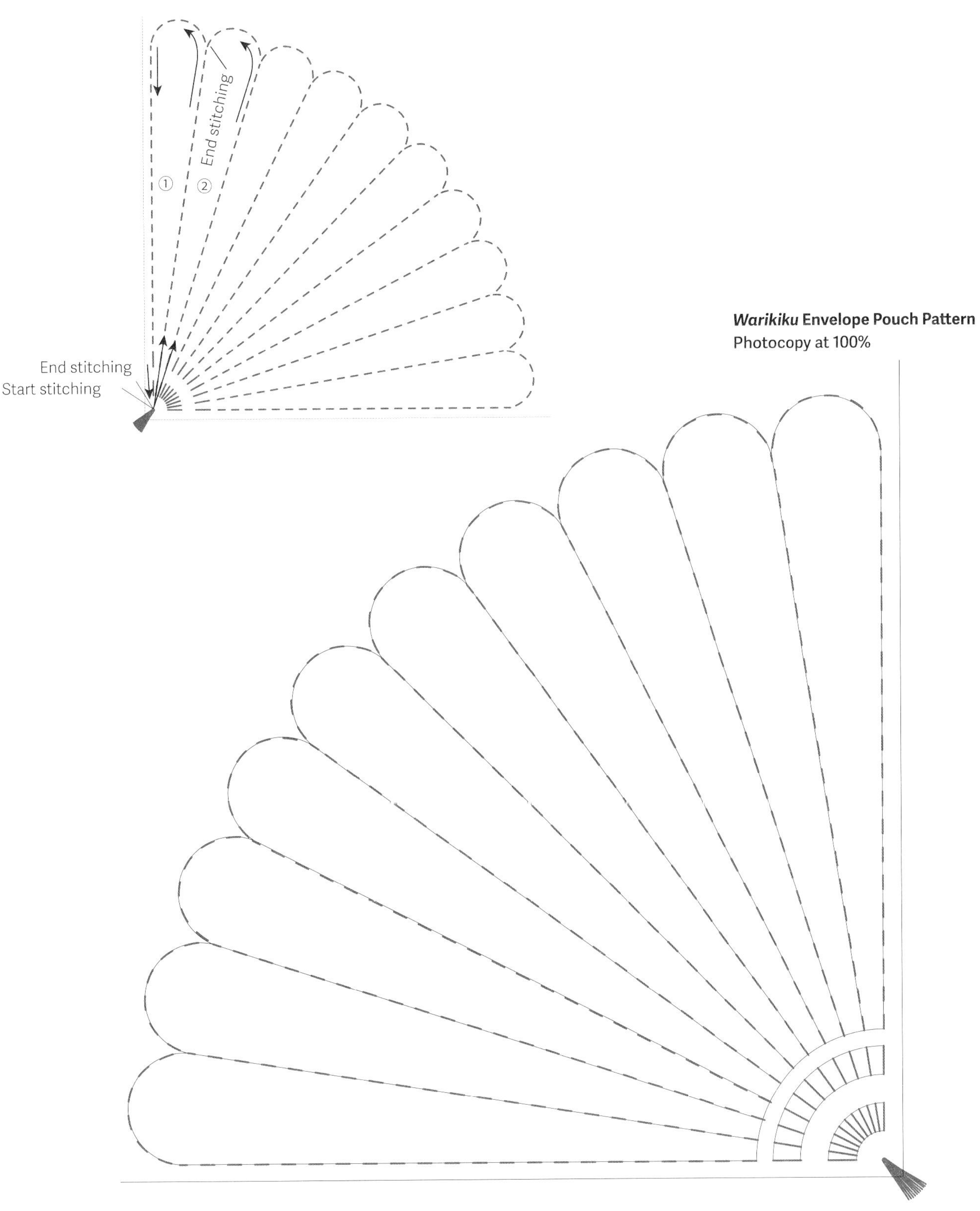

***Warikiku* Envelope Pouch Pattern**

Photocopy at 100%

PAGE 48 → MODERN DRAWSTRING BAGS

Finished size:
16 × 18cm

Materials (for one bag):
Outer fabric: 50 × 25cm
Lining fabric: 50 × 25cm
Cord: 0.5cm diameter, 100cm length
DARUMA Sashiko Thread (Thin) in colors: 202 (Ecru), 207 (Emerald), 214 (Carrot), 225 (Lapis Lazuli)

Tips:
- Add a 3cm seam allowance at the opening; add 1cm for all other edges.
- Pressing open the seam allowances at the sides helps keep the cord openings neat.
- For stitching methods, refer to page 57.

Instructions:
1. Do the sashiko stitching on the front outer piece.
2. Place the front and lining right sides together, and sew along the top. Repeat with the back and second lining fabric.
3. Open the units, then place so the front and back are right sides together and the linings are right sides together. Sew the sides and bottom, leaving openings for the cord and turning.
4. Turn it out, close the turning opening, and sew the channel for the cord.
5. Insert the cord and tie it.

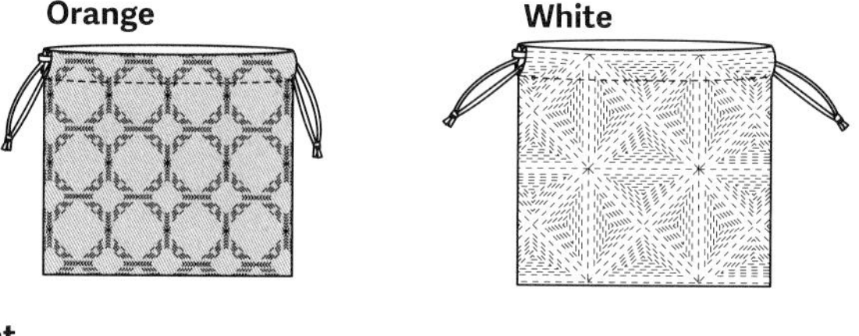

Orange Front (one piece)

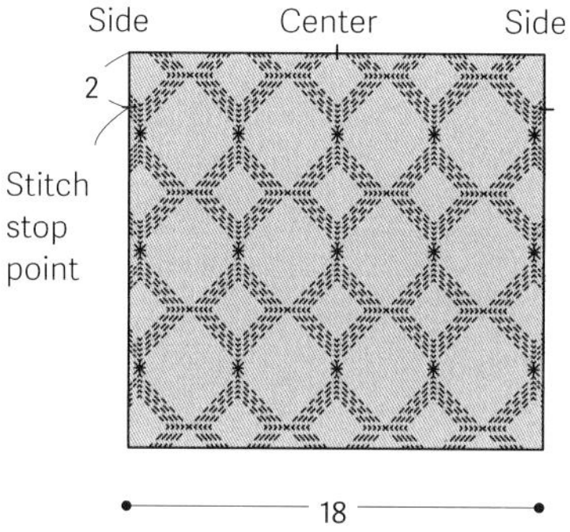

Side / Center / Side; 2; Stitch stop point; 16; 18

*Add a 3cm seam allowance at the opening.

White Front (one piece)

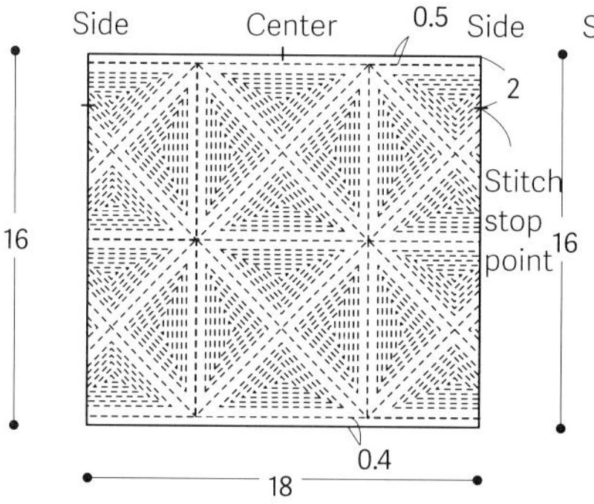

Side / Center / 0.5 / Side; 2; Stitch stop point; 16; 0.4; 18

*Add a 3cm seam allowance at the opening.

Back (one piece)

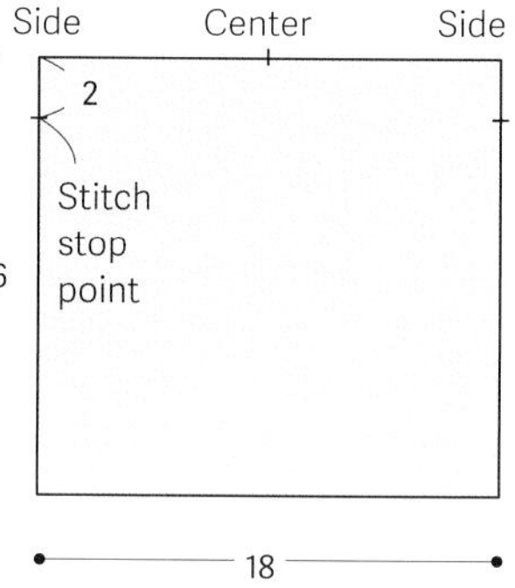

Side / Center / Side; 2; Stitch stop point; 18

*Add a 3cm seam allowance at the opening.

Lining (two pieces)

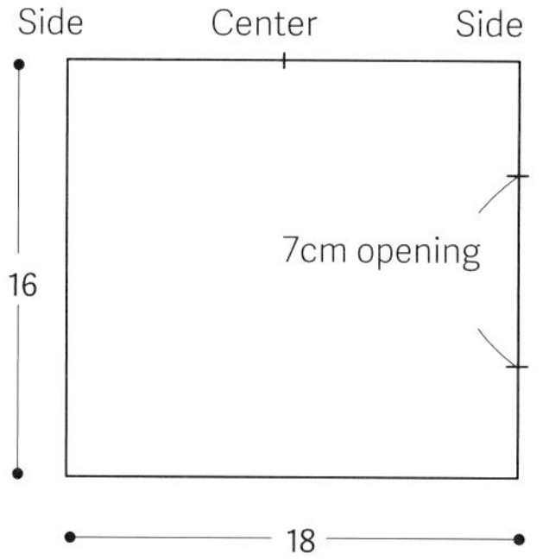

Side / Center / Side; 16; 7cm opening; 18

*Add a 3cm seam allowance at the opening.

How to Assemble

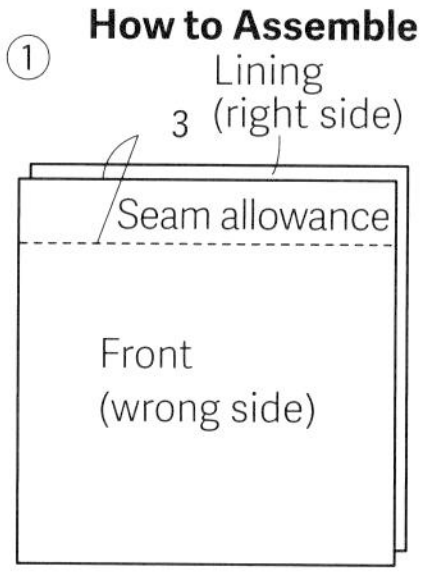

① Lining (right side); 3; Seam allowance; Front (wrong side)

Place an outer piece and lining right sides together, and sew the opening (top edge).

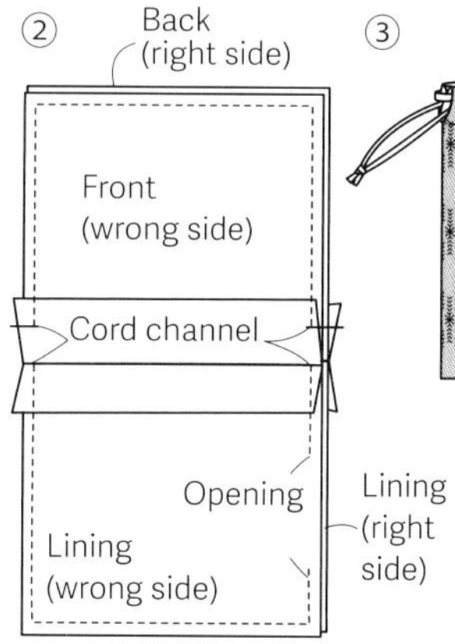

② Back (right side); Front (wrong side); Cord channel; Opening; Lining (wrong side); Lining (right side)

Open up step ①, then align the outer pieces and linings so that each pair is right sides together. Sew the sides and bottom, leaving openings for the cord and for turning.

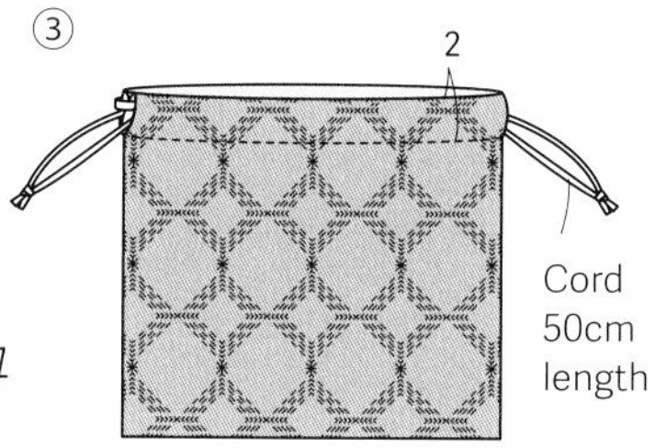

③ 2; Cord 50cm length

Turn it out, slip stitch the opening, sew the cord channel, and thread the cord through.

Orange Pattern
Photocopy at 100%

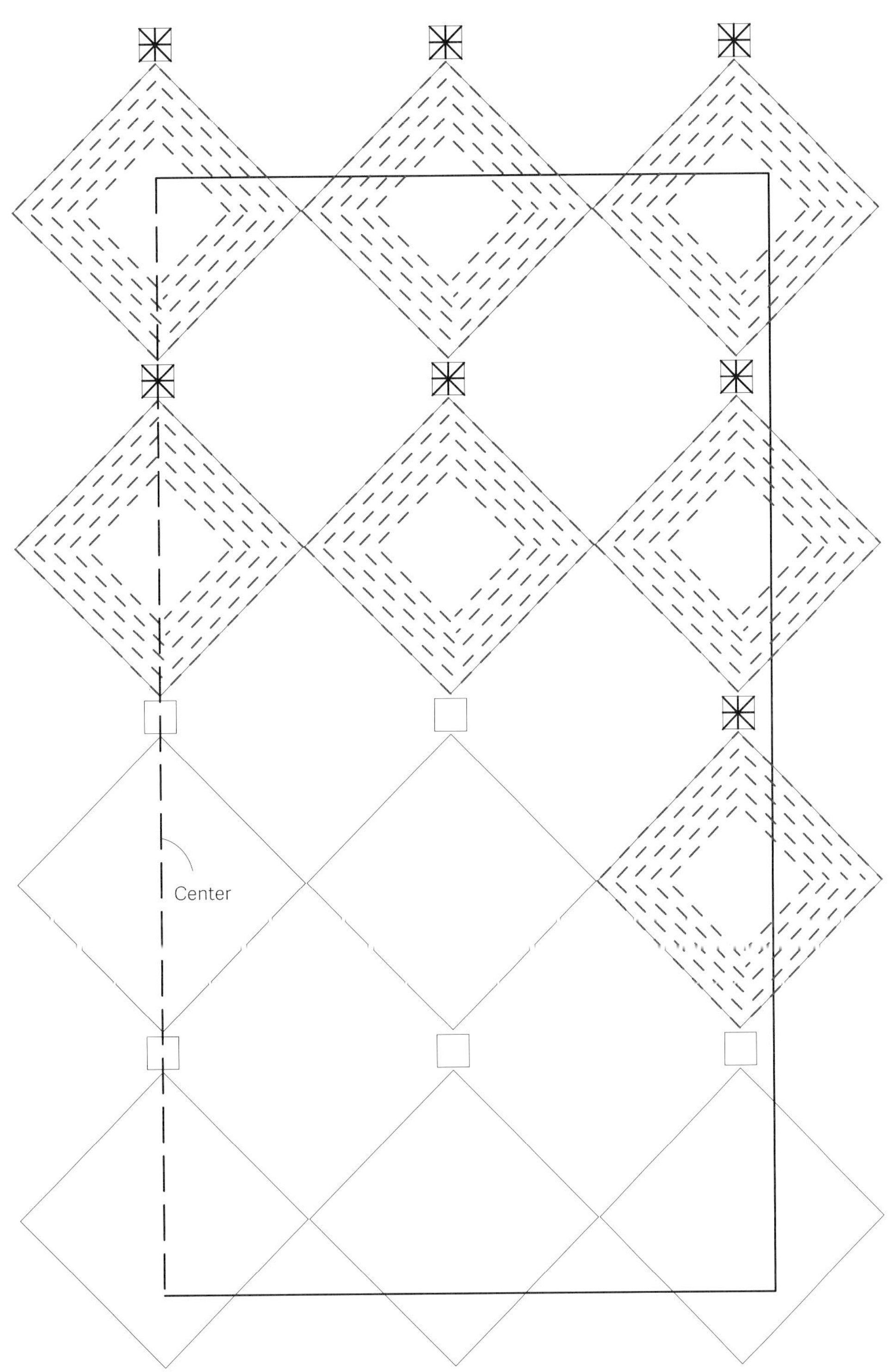

White Pattern
Photocopy at 100%

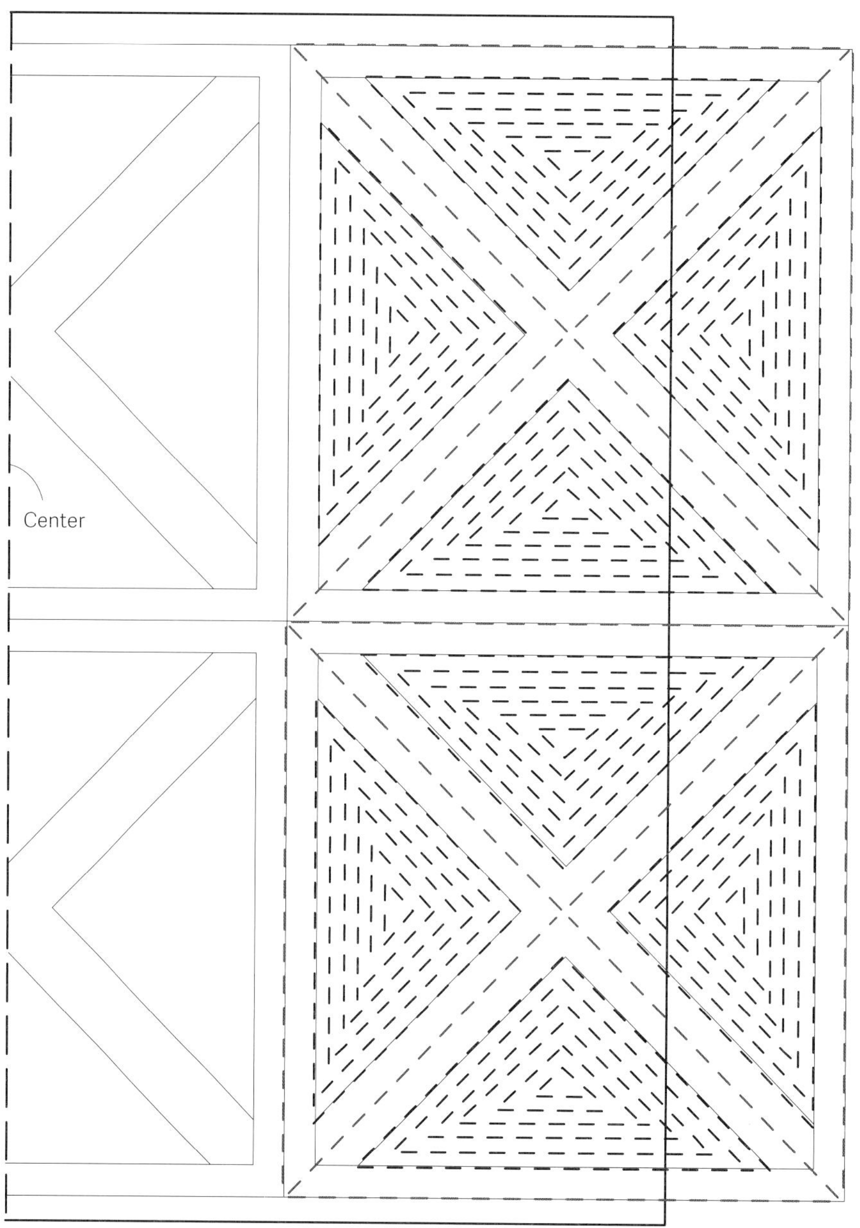

PAGE 62 → PLAID DRAWSTRING BAGS

Finished size:

16 × 18cm

Materials (for one bag):

Outer fabric (includes lining): 50 × 50cm
Cord: 0.4cm diameter, 100cm length
DARUMA Sashiko Thread (Thin) in colors: 208 (Bamboo) (white only), 221 (Madder)
COSMO Size 25 Embroidery Floss in colors: 578 (Gold), 2009 (Yellow) (green only)

Tips:

- Allow a 3cm seam allowance at the opening; use a 1cm seam allowance elsewhere.
- Pressing open the seam allowances at the sides helps keep the cord openings neat.
- For stitching methods, refer to page 67.
- Use three strands of the embroidery floss.

Instructions:

1. Do the sashiko stitching on the outer front piece.
2. Place the front and lining right sides together, and sew along the top. Repeat with the back and second lining fabric.
3. Open the units, then place so the front and back are right sides together and the linings are right sides together. Sew the sides and bottom, leaving openings for the cord and turning.
4. Turn it out, close the turning opening, and sew the channel for the cord.
5. Thread the cord and tie it.

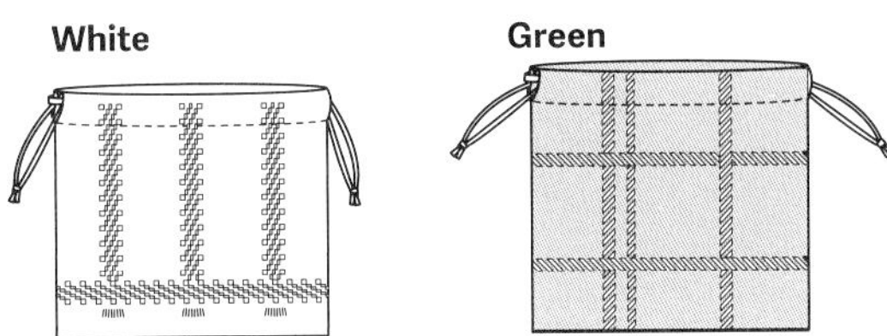

White Front (one piece)

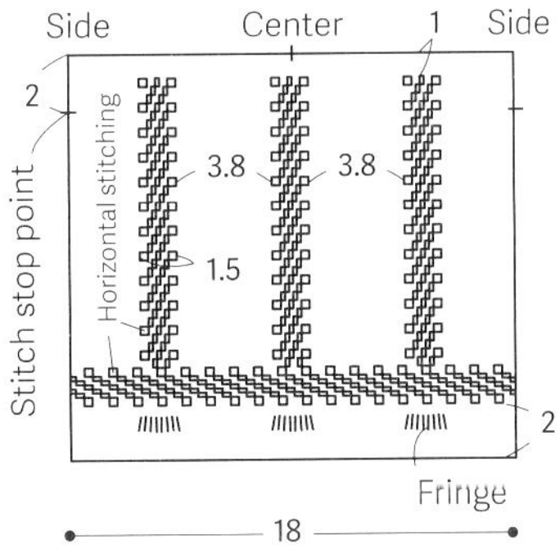

Side
Center
1
Side
2
Horizontal stitching
3.8
3.8
1.5
Stitch stop point
2
Fringe
18

*Add a 3cm seam allowance at the opening.

Green Front (one piece)

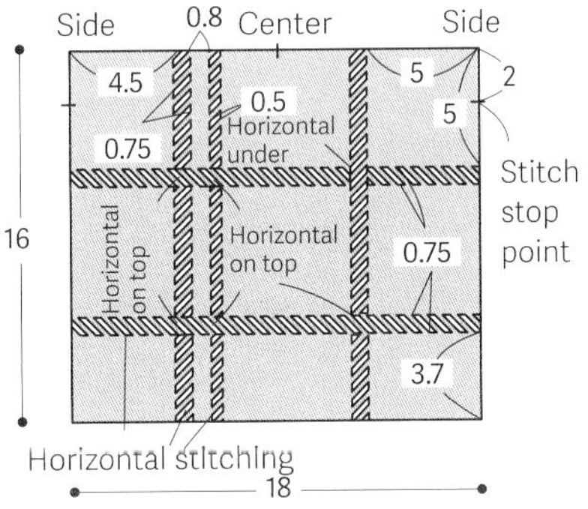

Side
0.8
Center
Side
4.5
0.5
Horizontal under
0.75
5
2
5
Stitch stop point
16
Horizontal on top
Horizontal on top
0.75
3.7
Horizontal stitching
18

*Add a 3cm seam allowance at the opening.

Back (one piece)

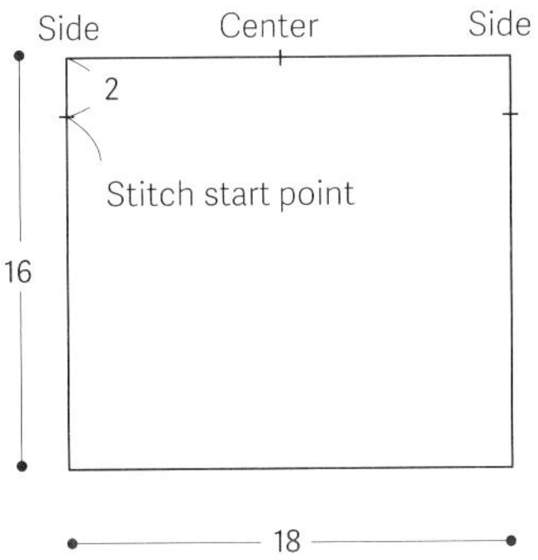

Side
Center
Side
2
Stitch start point
16
18

*Add a 3cm seam allowance at the opening.

Lining (two pieces)

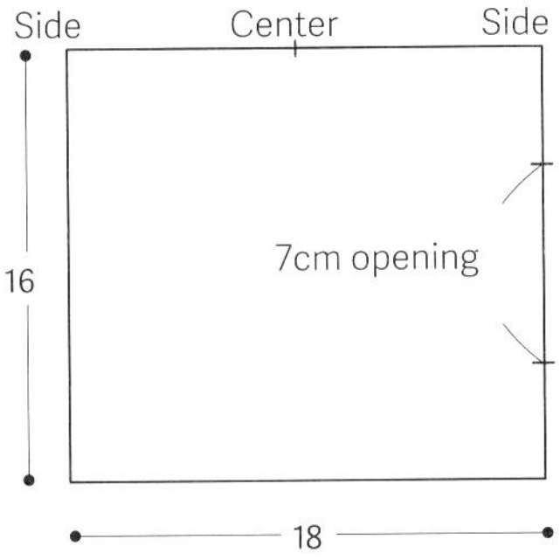

Side
Center
Side
16
7cm opening
18

*Add a 3cm seam allowance at the opening.

How to Assemble

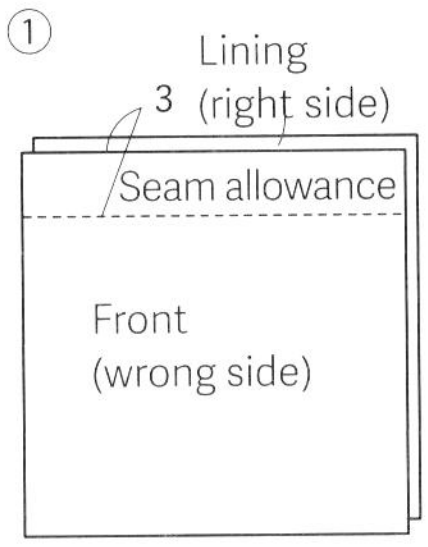

①
Lining
3 (right side)
Seam allowance
Front (wrong side)

Place an outer piece and lining right sides together, and sew opening (top edge).

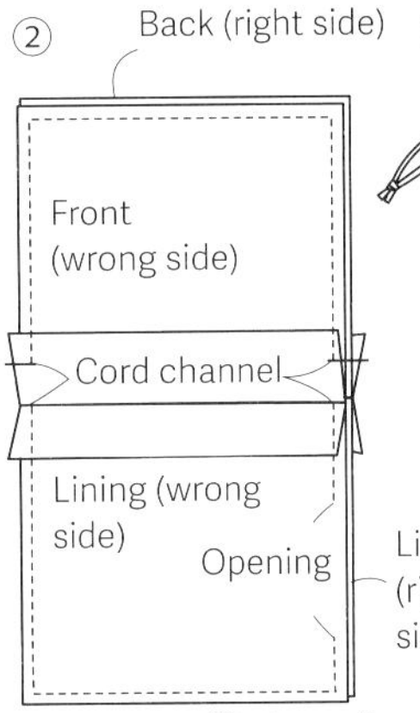

②
Back (right side)
Front (wrong side)
Cord channel
Lining (wrong side)
Opening
Lining (right side)

Open up step ①, then align the outer pieces and linings so that each pair is right sides together. Sew the sides and bottom, leaving openings for the cord and for turning.

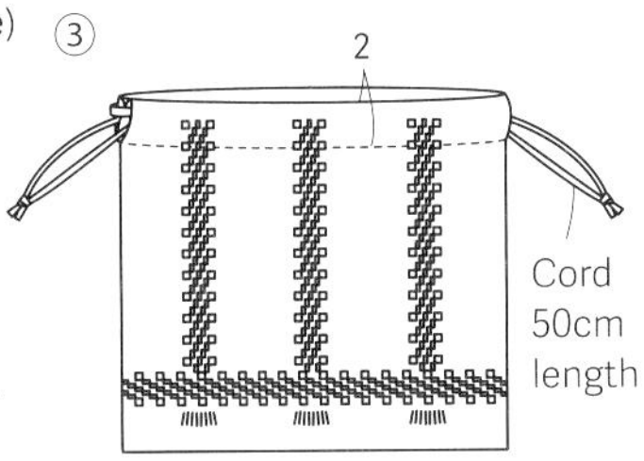

③
2
Cord 50cm length

Turn it out, slip stitch the opening, sew the cord channel, and thread the cord through.

Green Pattern
Photocopy at 100%

White Pattern
Photocopy at 100%

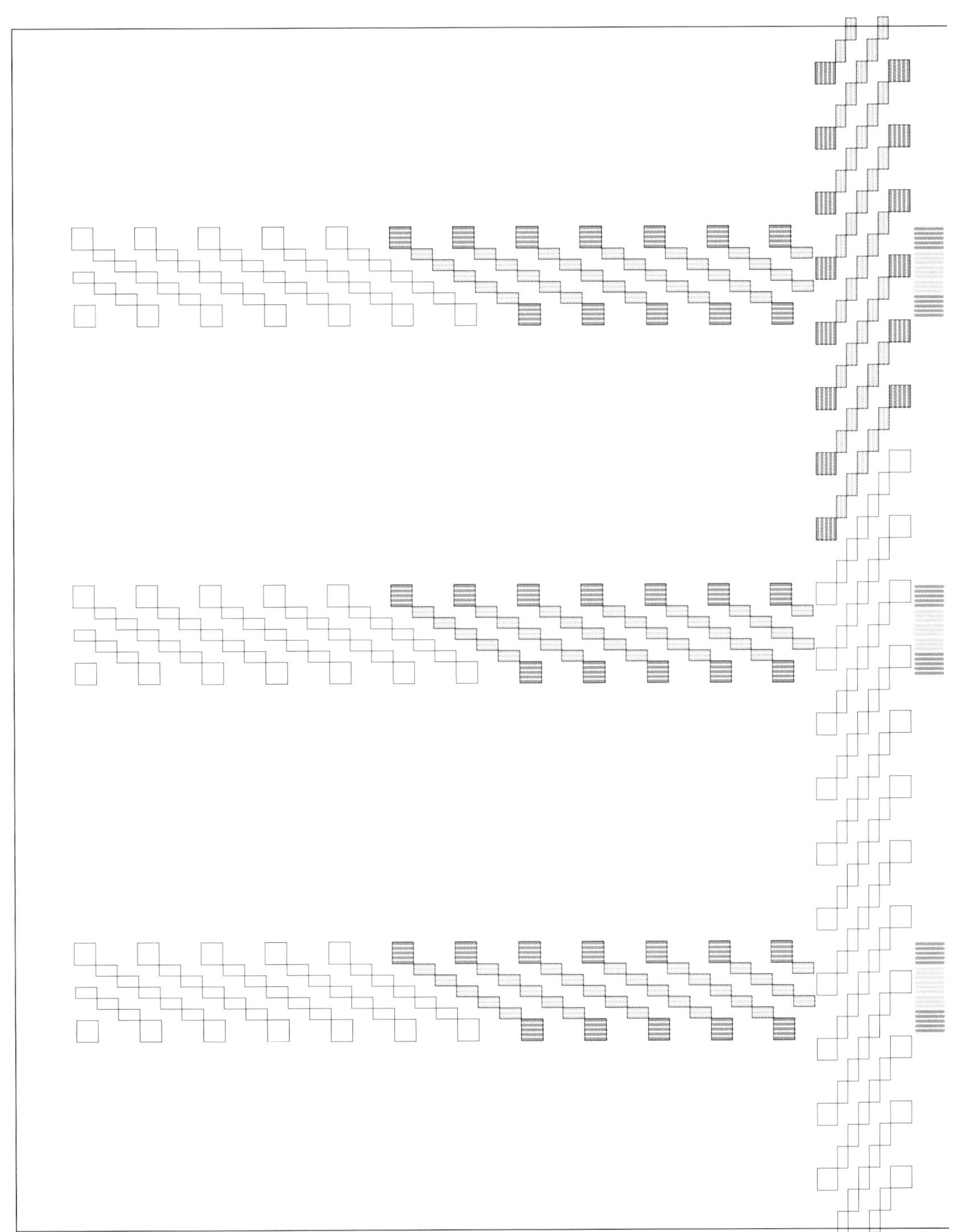

PAGE 50 → REVERSIBLE CLOTH:

Finished size:
46 × 45cm

Materials:
Outer fabric (two types): 50 × 50cm each
DARUMA Sashiko Thread (Thick) in colors: 202 (Ecru), 215 (Navy Blue)

Tip:
- Leave the beginning and end of the sashiko thread loose to form fringes.

Instructions:
1. Place the two outer pieces right sides together and sew around the edges, leaving an opening for turning.
2. Turn it right side out and slip stitch the opening closed.
3. Do the sashiko embroidery.

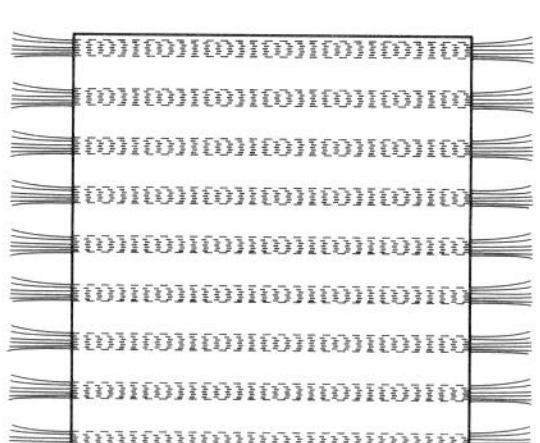

Outer Layer (two pieces)

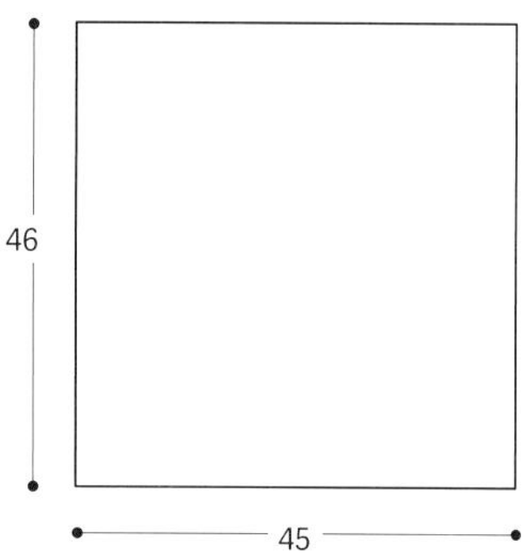

How to Assemble

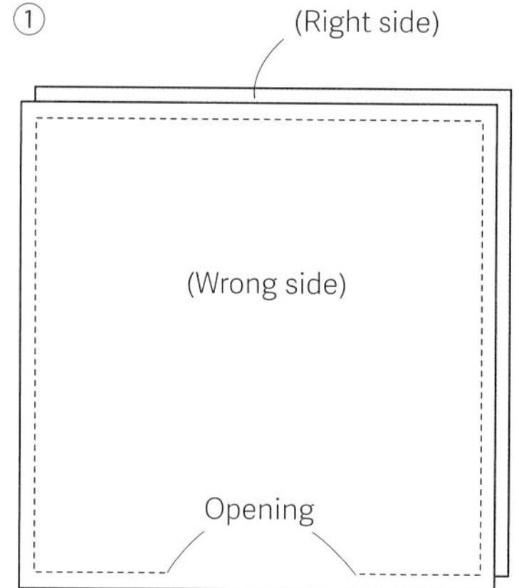

Place the pieces right sides together, leaving an opening, and sew around the edges.

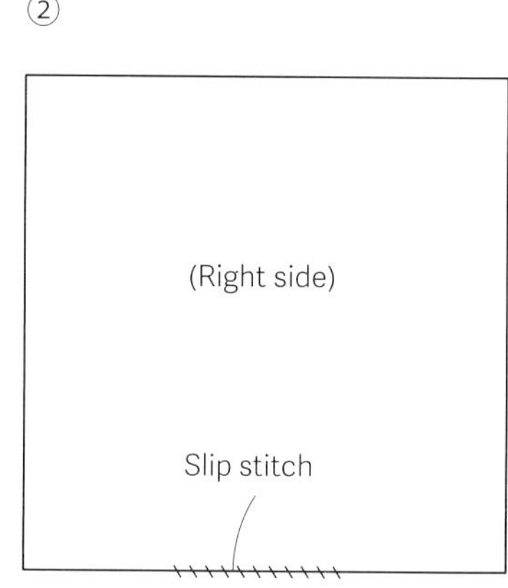

Turn it right side out and slip stitch the opening closed.

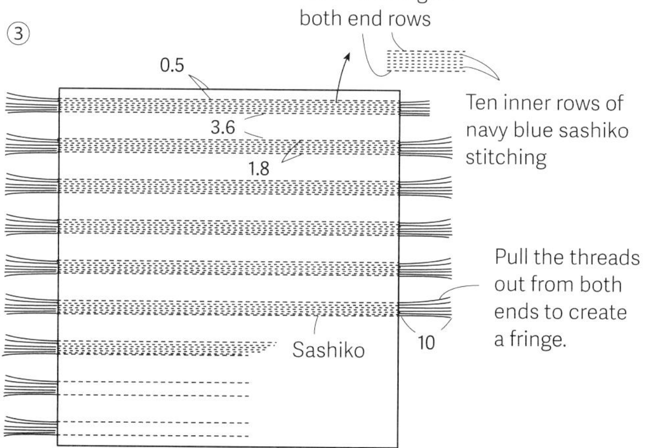

PAGE 59 → MONOTONE PLACE MAT

Finished size:
35 × 47cm

Materials:
Outer fabric: 110 × 40cm
Inner fabric: 100 × 80cm
COSMO Size 25 Embroidery Floss in color: 601 (Neutral)
DARUMA Home Thread (Thin) in color: Off-White

Tips:
- For stitching methods, refer to pages 66–67.
- Use two layers of inner fabric for the kantha quilting. Adjust the number and size of layers depending on the fabric.
- Use all six strands of the embroidery floss.

Instructions:
1. Place the two outer fabric pieces right sides together, layer the inner fabric below, and sew around the edges leaving an opening for turning.
2. Turn right side out and slip stitch the opening closed.
3. Do horizontal stitching first, then proceed with kantha quilting.

Outer Layer (two pieces)

How to Assemble

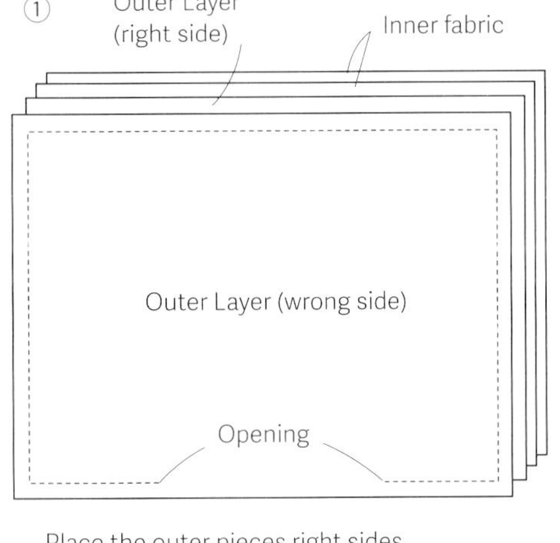

Place the outer pieces right sides together, leaving an opening, and sew around the edges.

2

0.7
Kantha quilting
Leave the thread ends exposed on both sides of the stitching.
0.7
3
Horizontal stitching
Slip stitch
1.5
0.7

Use six strands of embroidery floss.

Turn it right side out, and slip stitch the opening closed. Stitch the horizontal lines first, then do the kantha quilting.

Monotone Place Mat Pattern
Photocopy at 100%

PAGE 52 → VARIOUS PINCUSHIONS

Finished sizes:

A: 4.5 × 7cm
B: 5.5 × 6.5cm
C: 5.5 × 6.5cm
D: 5.5 × 6.5cm
E: 6.5 × 6.5cm
F: 6.5 × 7.5cm

Materials (for one pincushion):

Outer fabric: 20 × 10cm
Appliqué fabric: 10 × 10cm (F only)
Craft stuffing, as needed
DARUMA Sashiko Thread (Thick) in colors: 202 (Ecru), 215 (Navy Blue)

Tips:

- For stitching methods, refer to pages 40–41.
- Stitch freely.

Instructions:

1. Do sashiko stitching on the front piece.
2. Place the front and back pieces right sides together and sew around the edges, leaving an opening.
3. Turn it right side out, stuff, and slip stitch the opening closed.

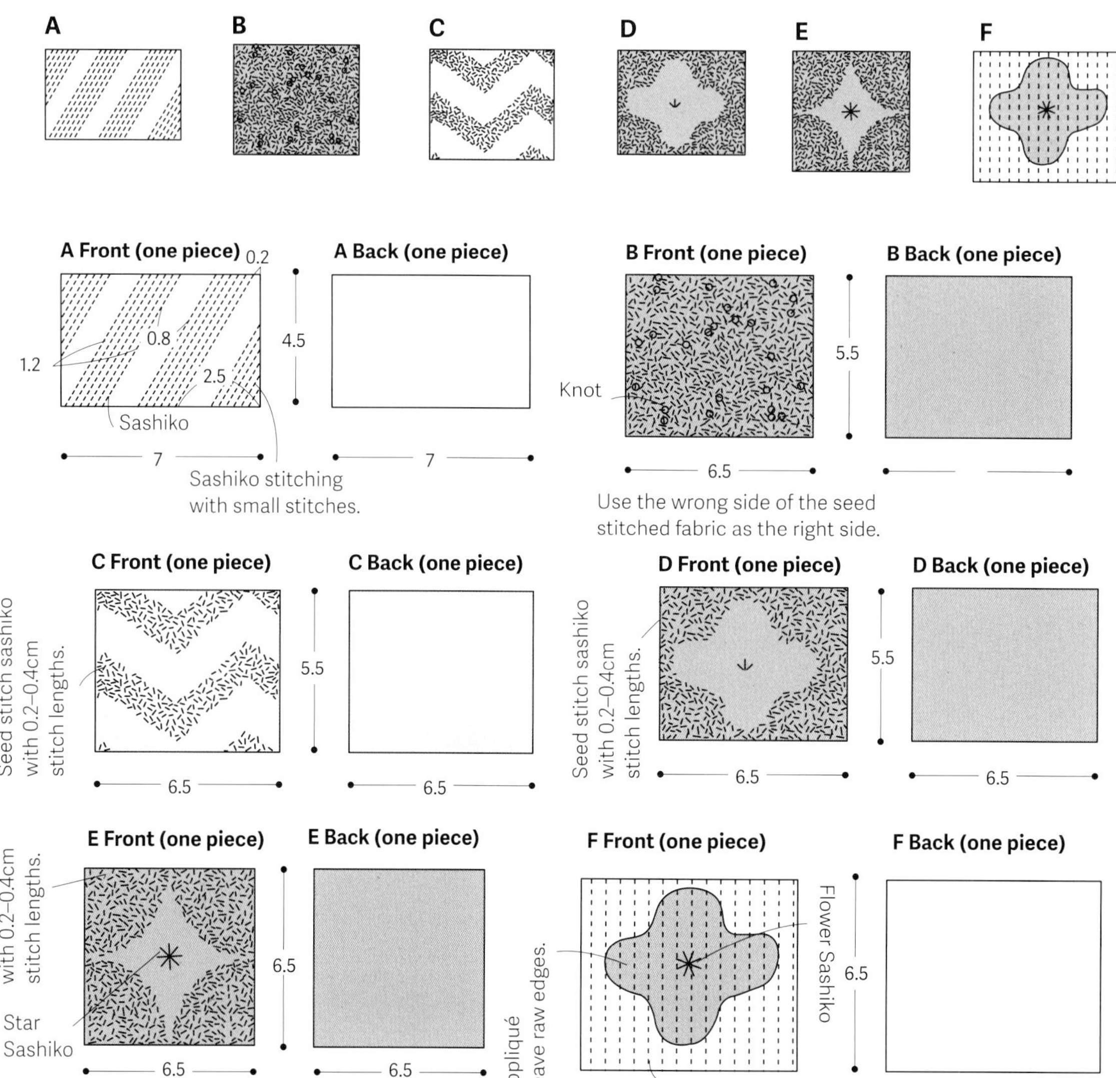

How to Assemble

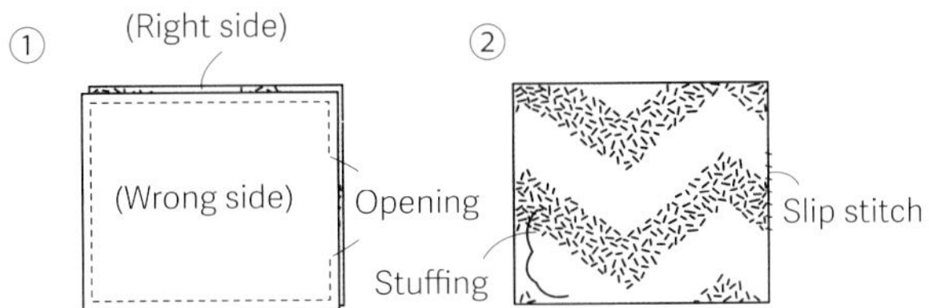

Place the front and back pieces right sides together and sew around the edges, leaving an opening.

Turn it right side out, stuff, and slip stitch the opening closed.

C–F Patterns
Photocopy at 100%

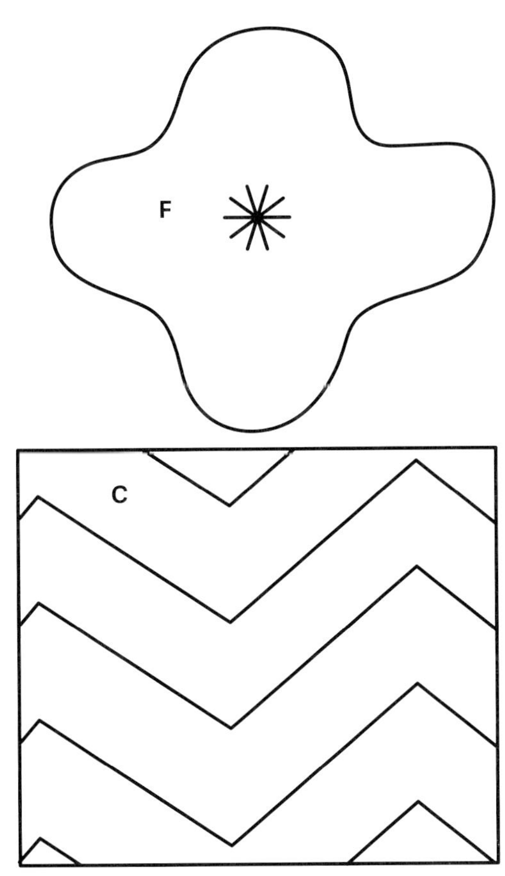

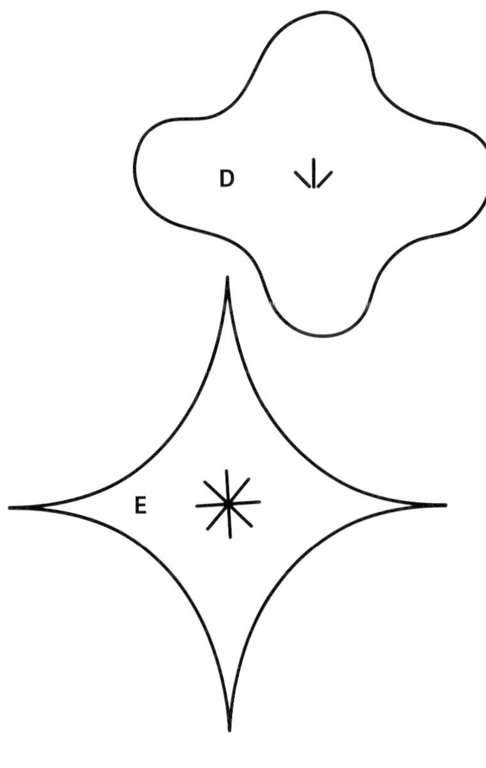

Finished size:
9 × 9 × 9cm

Materials (for one sachet):
Outer fabric: 25 × 15cm
Cord: 1cm diameter, 20cm length
Potpourri, as needed
DARUMA Sashiko Thread (Thick) in colors: 219 (Black), 228 (Warbler)

Tips:
- For stitching methods, refer to page 67.
- Use one strand of black thread and two strands of Warbler (yellowish green) thread for stitching.

Instructions:
1. Do the sashiko stitching.
2. Fold the fabric in half with right sides together and sew two sides.
3. Turn it right side out, fill with potpourri, and close the opening using a ladder stitch (invisible stitch).
4. Make the cord and sew it to the tip of the sachet.

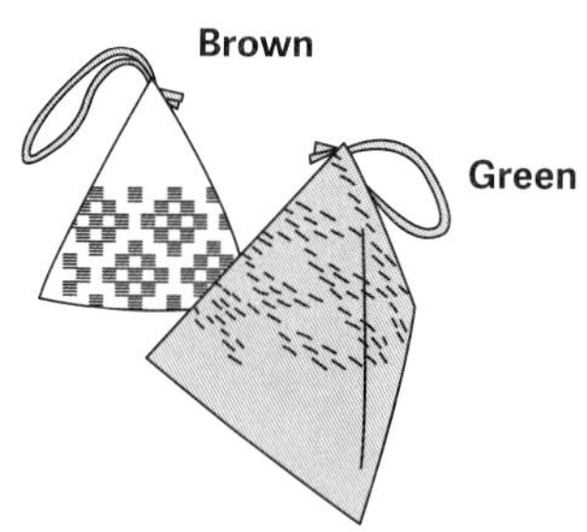

Brown Front (one piece)

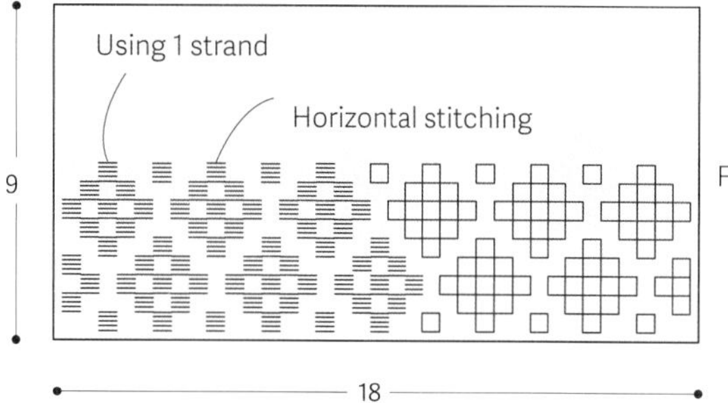

How to Assemble

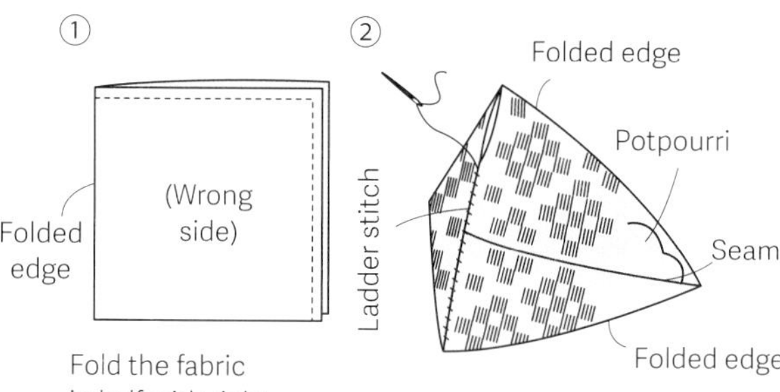

① Fold the fabric in half with right sides together and sew two sides.

② Turn it right side out, fill it with potpourri or other stuffing, and close the opening using ladder stitch.

Green Front (one piece)

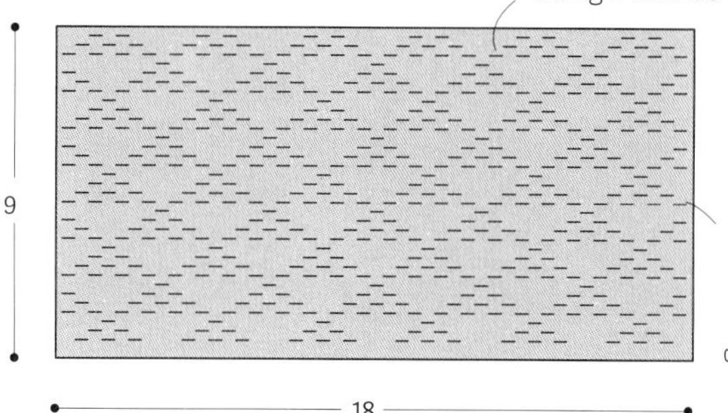

Cord (two pieces)

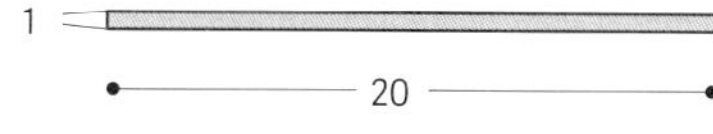

How to Make the Cord

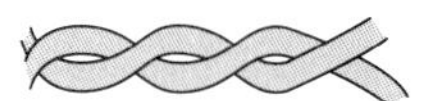

Wrap two cords around each other.

How to Attach the Cord

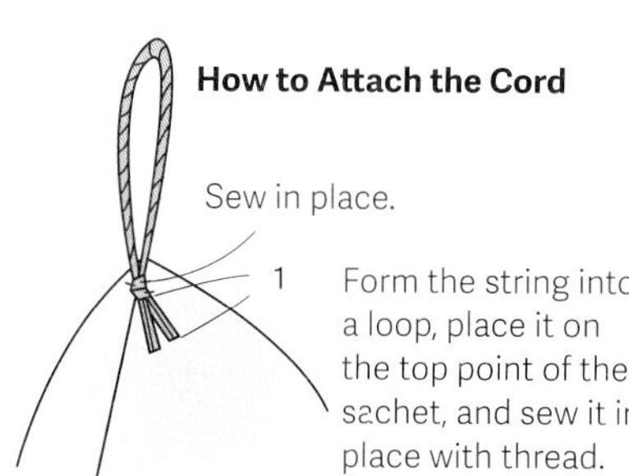

Form the string into a loop, place it on the top point of the sachet, and sew it in place with thread.

Brown Pattern
Photocopy at 100%

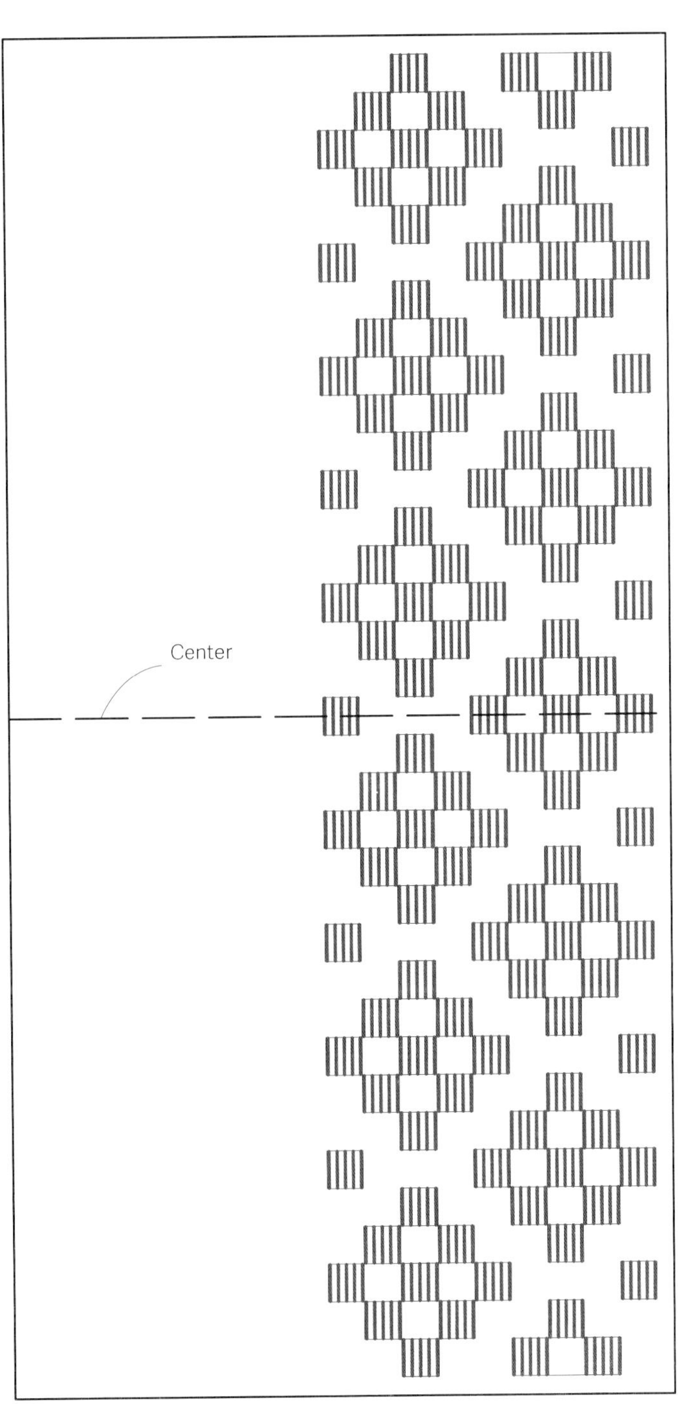

Green Pattern
Photocopy at 100%

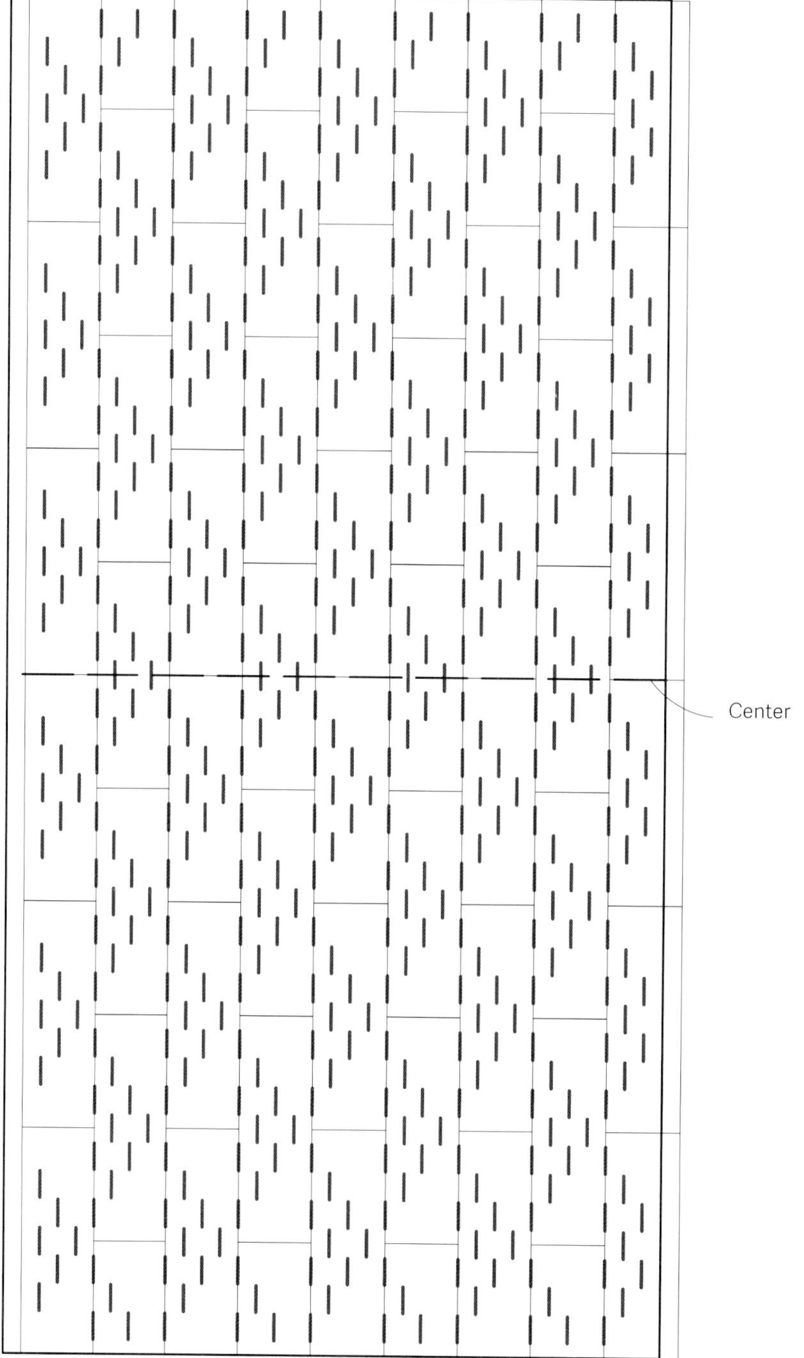

PAGE 70 → LATTICE BASKET COVER

Finished size:

22.5 × 29cm

Materials:

Outer fabric: 70 × 30cm
DARUMA Sashiko Thread (Thick) in color: 219 (Black)

Tip:

- For stitching methods, refer to page 77.

Instructions:

1. Do sashiko stitching on the front fabric.
2. With right sides together, sew the front and back together, leaving an opening.
3. Turn it right side out and slip stitch the opening closed.

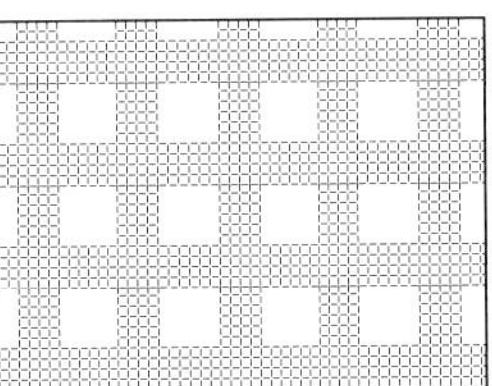

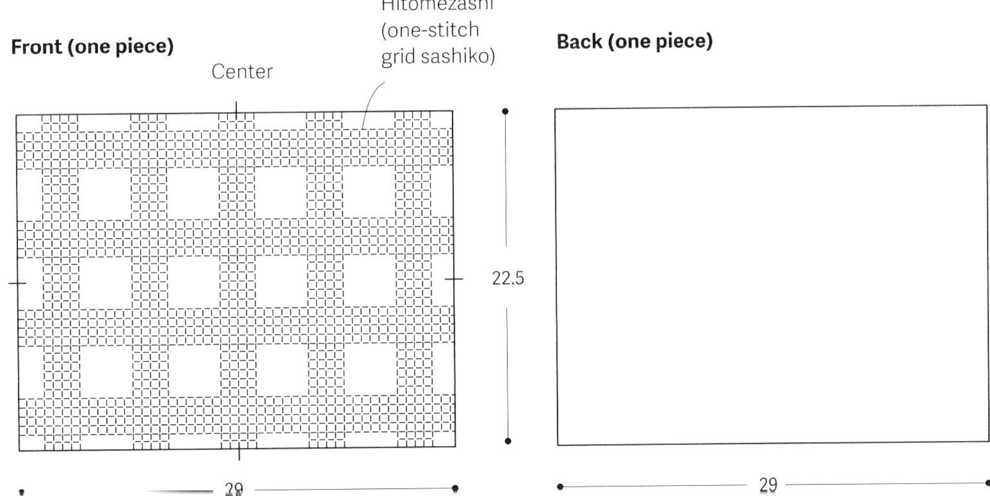

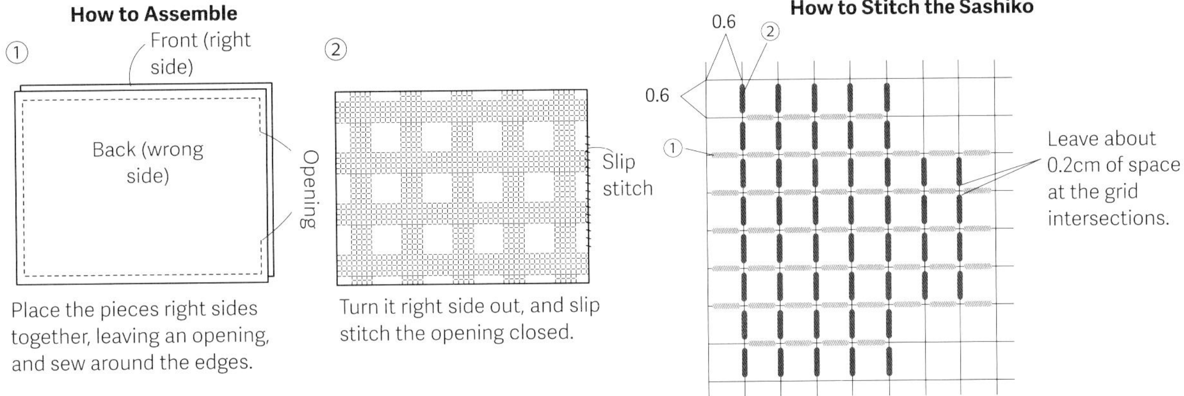

Draw a grid with 0.6cm spacing from the center, then do the horizontal sashiko stitching for step ①. Next, do the vertical sashiko stitching for step ②.

PAGE 64 → *SUGIZASHI* POT HOLDER

Finished size:
16 × 16cm

Materials (for one pot holder):
Outer fabric: 40 × 20cm
Loop fabric: 15 × 5cm
Inner fabric: 40 × 40cm
Batting: 20 × 20cm
DARUMA Sashiko Thread (Thick) in color: 202 (Ecru)

Tips:

- For stitching methods, refer to page 67.
- Use three to four layers of inner fabric. Adjust the number and size of layers depending on the fabric used.

Instructions:

1. Do the sashiko stitching on the front fabric.
2. Make the loop.
3. Place the front and back fabric right sides together. Layer the inner fabric and batting, and sew around the edges, leaving an opening for turning. Insert the loop at this stage.
4. Turn it right side out and slip stitch the opening closed.

Front (one piece)

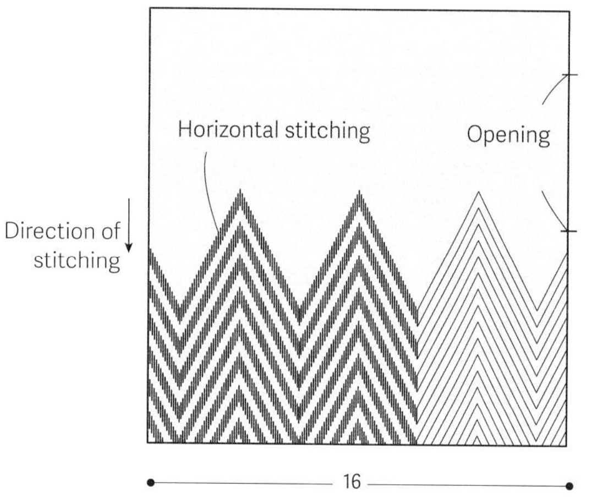

Back (one piece)

Loop (one piece)

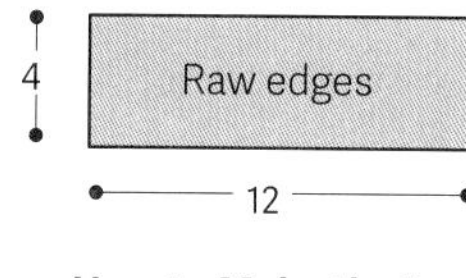

How to Make the Loop

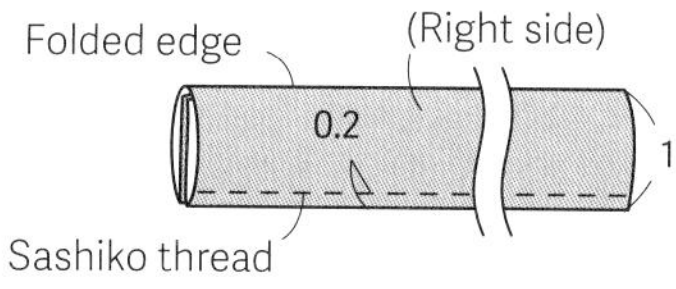

Fold into four and sew the edges.

How to Assemble

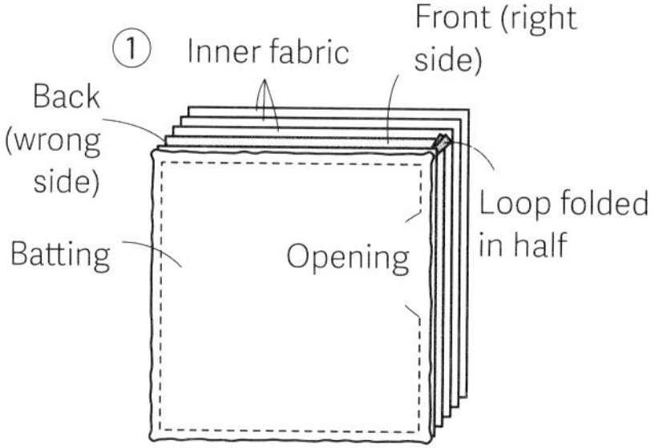

Place the front and back right sides together, layer three to four pieces of inner fabric and one layer of batting, insert the loop, and sew around the edges, leaving an opening.

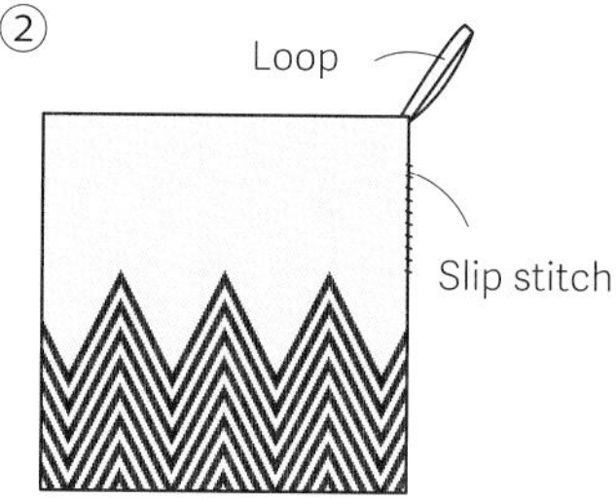

Turn it right side out and slip stitch the opening closed.

***Sugizashi* Pot Holder Pattern**
Photocopy at 100%

PAGE 69 → INDIGO MINI MATS

Finished sizes:
A: 11.5 × 17cm
B: 14 × 19cm

Materials:
A:
Outer fabric: 40 × 15cm
Inner fabric: 20 × 15cm
DARUMA Sashiko Thread (Thick) in color: 229 (Grey)
B:
Appliqué fabric scraps
Base fabric: 20 × 15cm
DARUMA Sashiko Thread (Thick) in color: 229 (Grey)
DARUMA Sashiko Thread (Thin) in colors: 202 (Ecru), 215 (Navy Blue), 226 (Water Blue)

Tip:
- For stitching methods, refer to page 77.

Instructions:
A:
1. Do sashiko stitching on the front fabric.
2. With the front and back fabric right sides together, layer the inner fabric on top. Sew around the edges, leaving an opening for turning.
3. Turn it right side out and slip stitch the opening closed.

B:
1. Layer the appliqué fabric on the base fabric and do sashiko stitching.

A

B

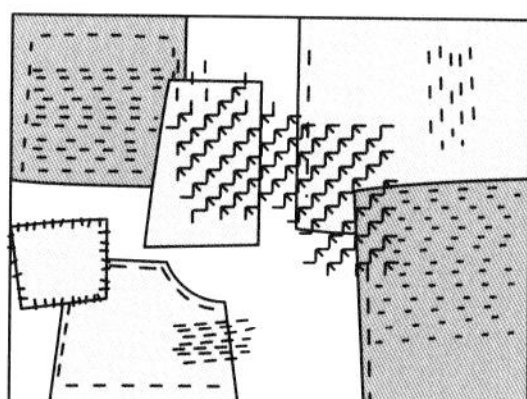

A Front (one piece)

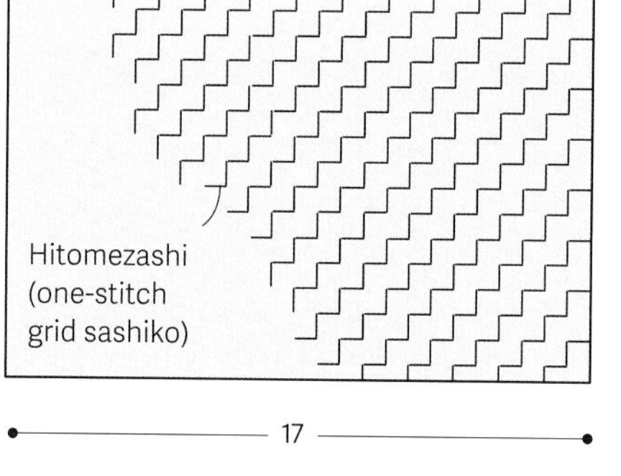

A Back (one piece)

B Base Layer (one piece)

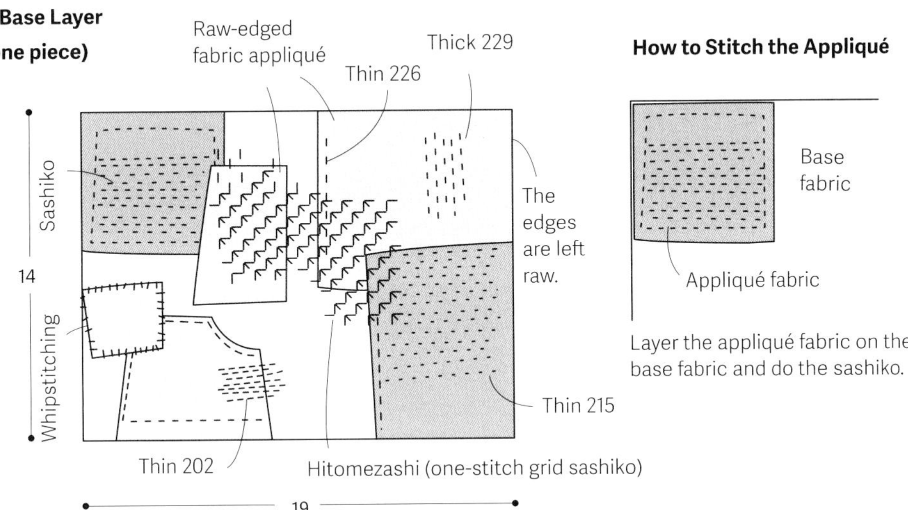

How to Stitch the Appliqué

Base fabric

Appliqué fabric

Layer the appliqué fabric on the base fabric and do the sashiko.

How to Assemble A

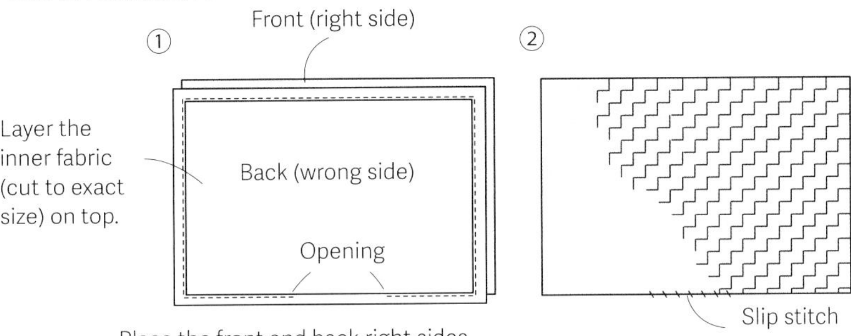

Place the front and back right sides together, layer the inner fabric, and sew around the edges, leaving an opening.

Turn it right side out, slip stitch the opening closed.

How to Stitch the Sashiko

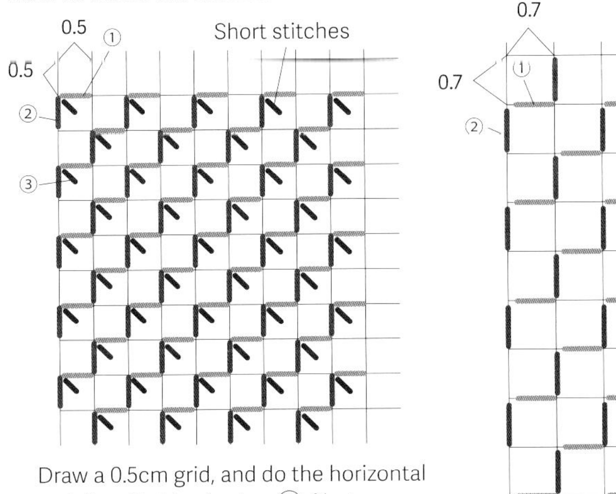

Draw a 0.5cm grid, and do the horizontal sashiko stitching in step ①. Next, do the vertical sashiko stitching in step ②, and finally, do the diagonal sashiko stitching in step ③.

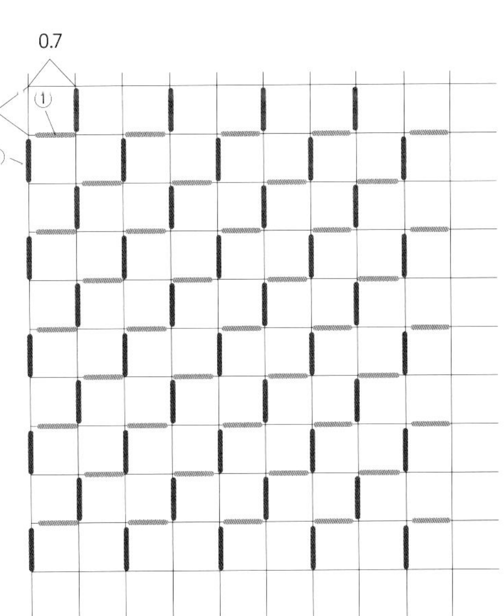

Draw a 0.7cm grid, and do the horizontal sashiko stitching in step ①. Next, do the vertical sashiko stitching in step ②.

PAGE 72 → PATTERNED WALL HANGING

Finished size:
55 × 45cm

Materials:
Base fabric: 45 × 60cm
DARUMA Sashiko Thread (Thick) in color: 215 (Navy Blue)

Tip:
- For stitching methods, refer to pages 76–77. Begin stitching from the bottom-left area.

Instructions:
1. Do sashiko stitching on the base fabric.
2. Sew the hanging sleeve.

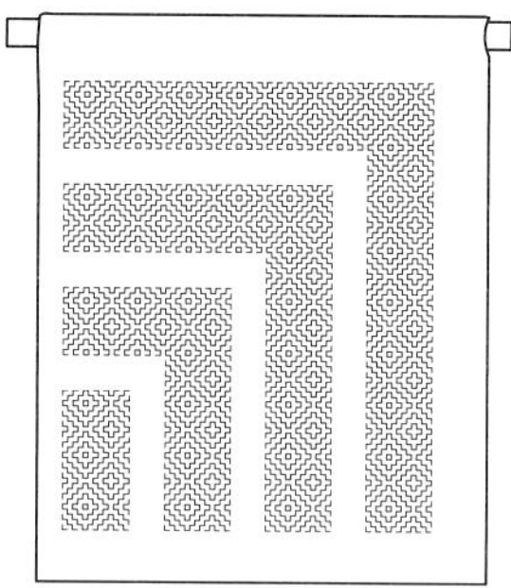

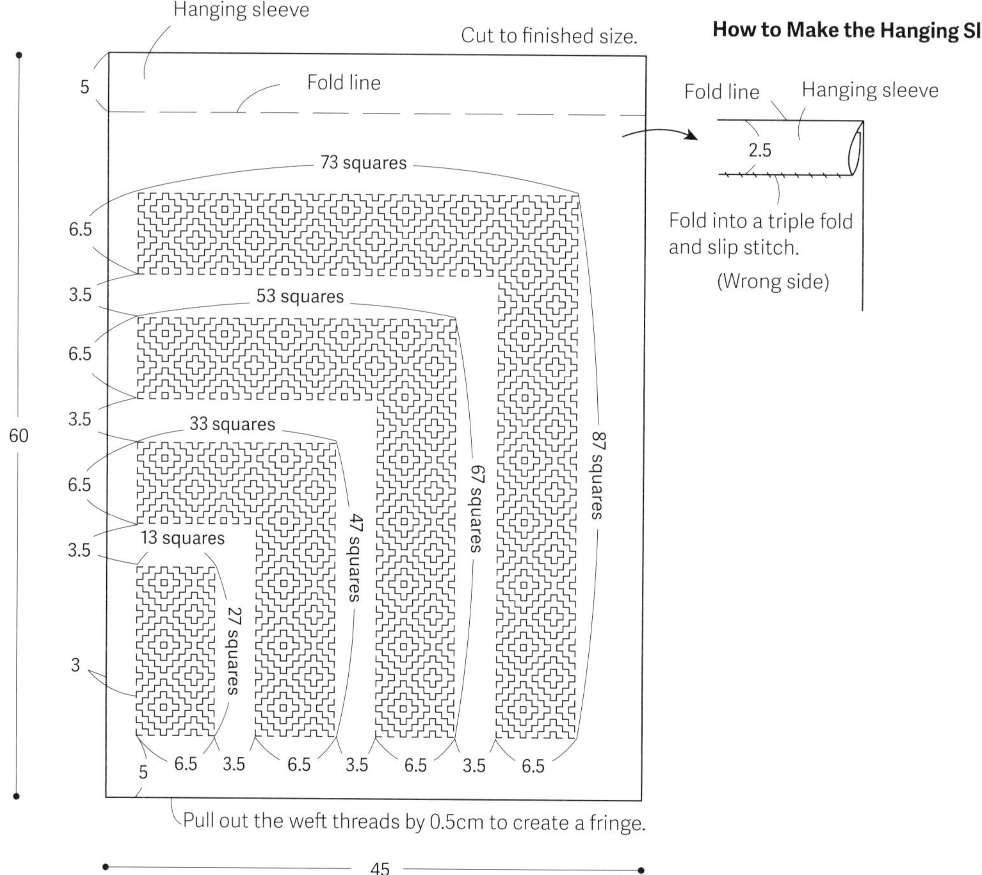

How to Stitch the Sashiko

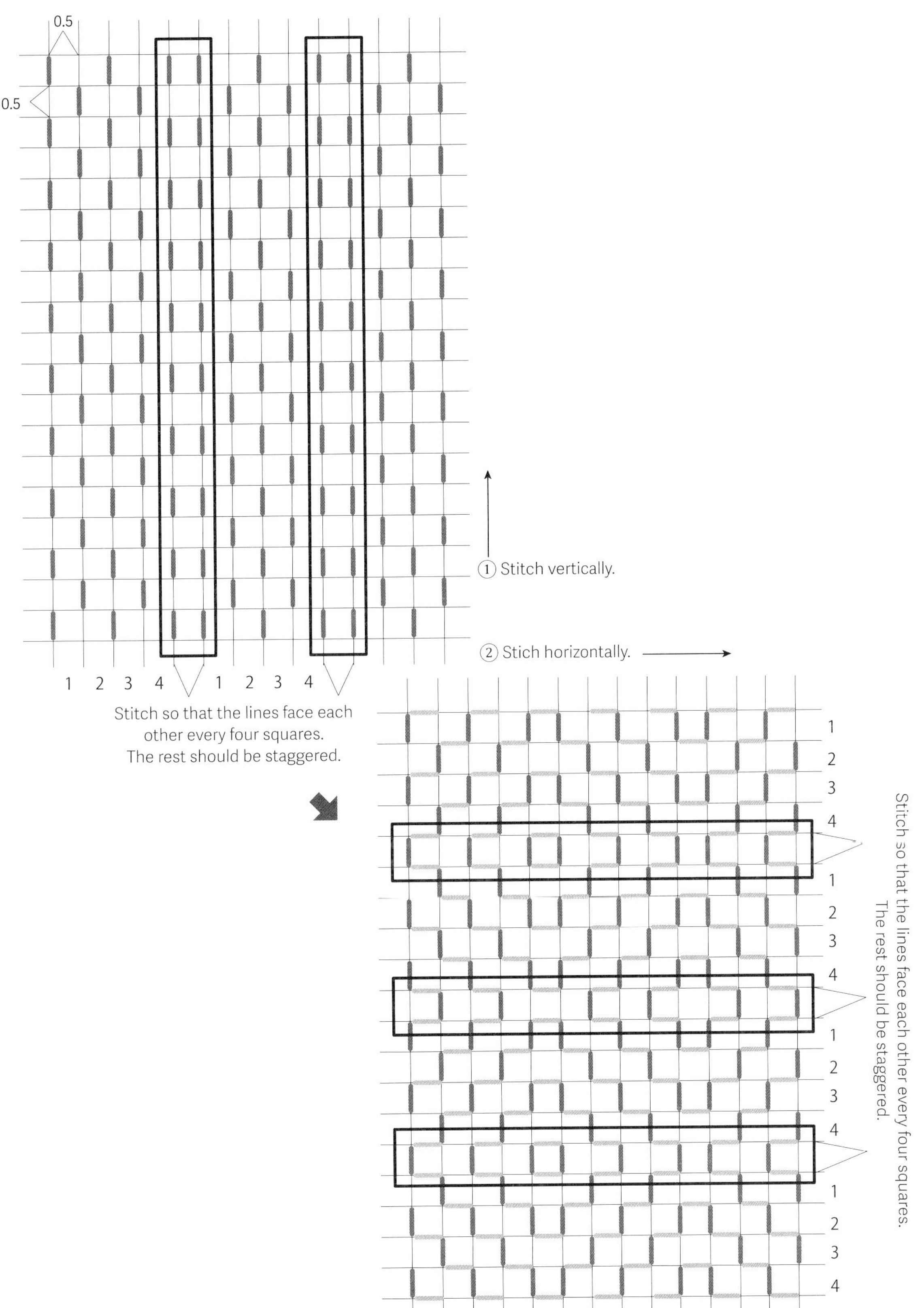

Finished sizes:
Pink: 90.5 × 90.5cm
White: 80 × 91cm

Materials:
Pink:
Main fabric: 85 × 170cm
Border fabric: 100 × 65cm
DARUMA Sashiko Thread (Thick) in color: 205 (Peacock)
White:
Main fabric: 100 × 170cm
Border fabric: 90 × 60cm
DARUMA Sashiko Thread (Thick) in color: 229 (Grey)

Tips:
- When slip stitching the border fabric on the back, avoid letting the stitches show on the front.
- For stitching methods, refer to pages 76–77.

Instructions:
1. Layer two pieces of the main fabric, wrong sides together, and attach the border fabric around the edges.
2. Fold the border fabric to the back and slip stitch in place.
3. For the pink version, do sashiko on the border area. For the white version, do sashiko around the main fabric edges.

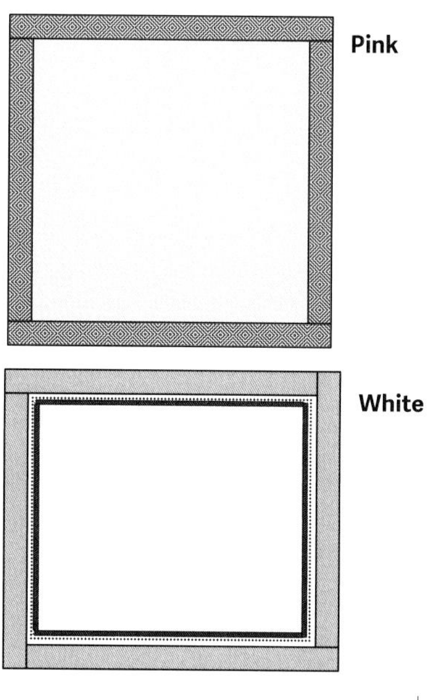

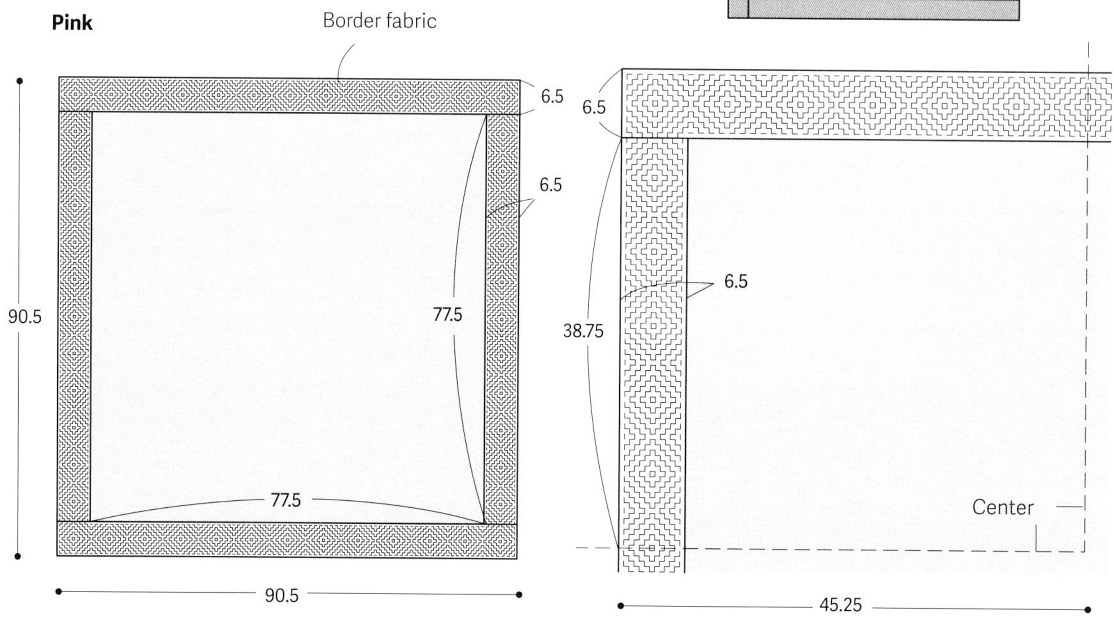

Front & Back (one piece each)

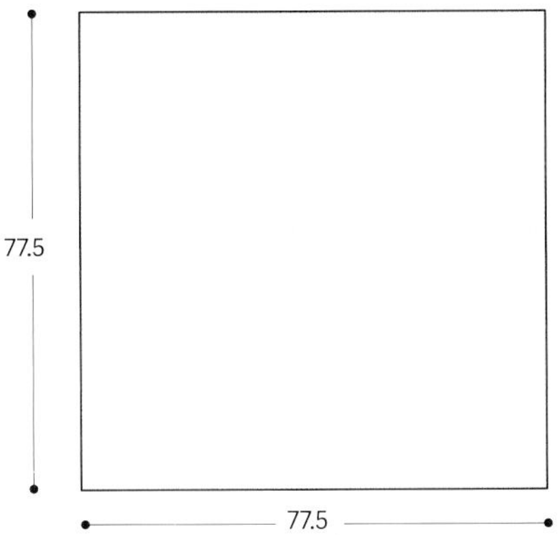

77.5

77.5

Border A (two pieces)

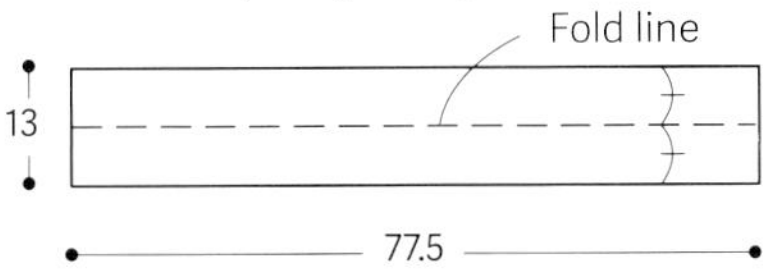

Fold line

13

77.5

Border B (two pieces)

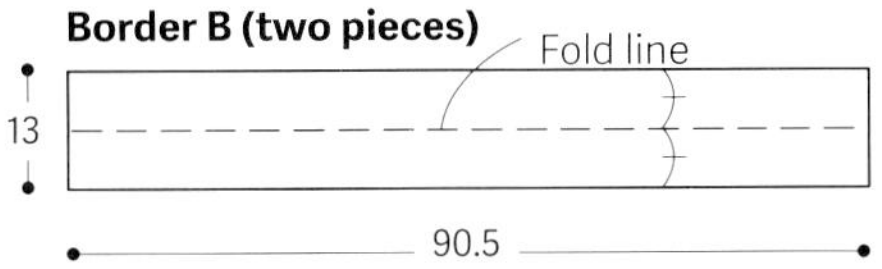

Fold line

13

90.5

How to Assemble Pink

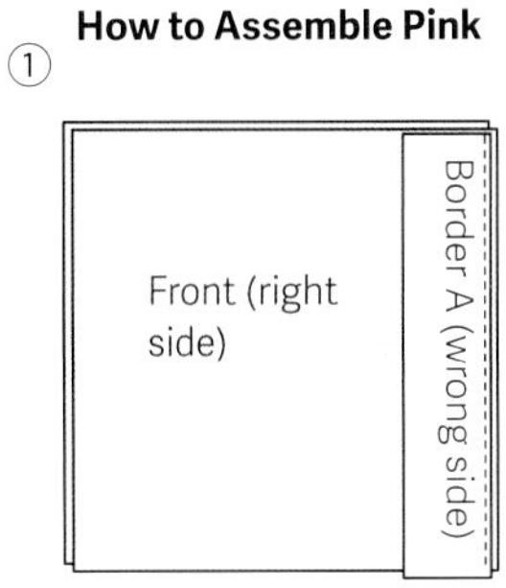

①

Front (right side)

Border A (wrong side)

Layer the front and back with the right sides facing out, and sew a border A to both sides with right sides together.

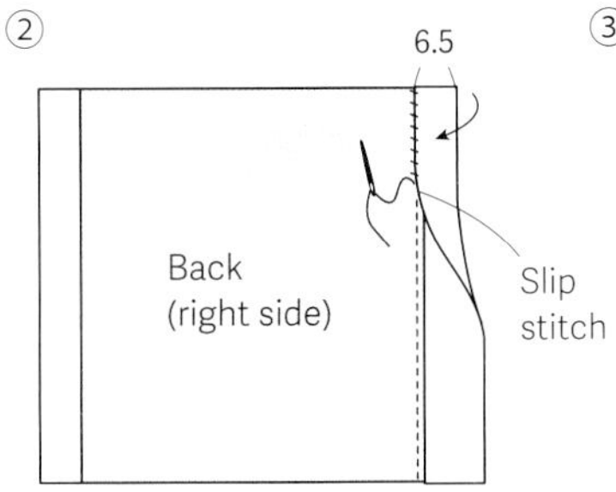

②

6.5

Back (right side)

Slip stitch

Fold the border fabric to the back and slip stitch it in place so that the stitches don't show on the front.

③

Border B (wrong side)

Front (right side)

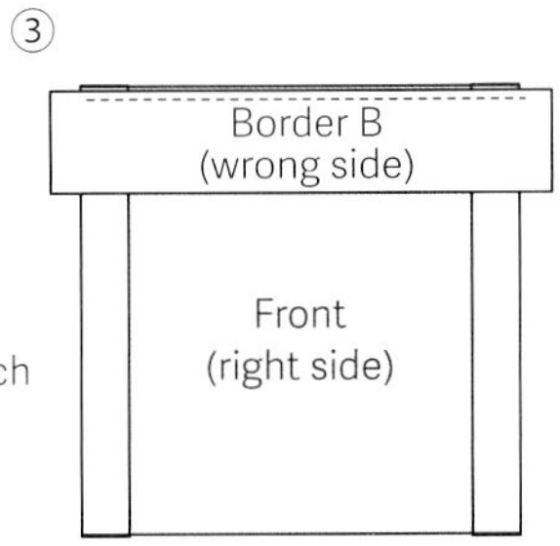

Sew a border B to the top and bottom, right sides together.

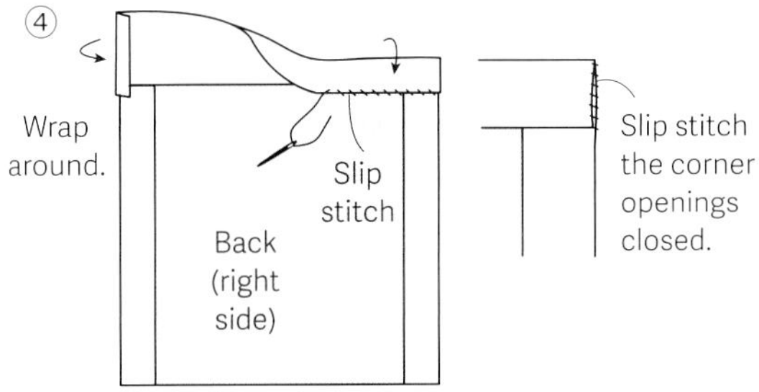

④

Wrap around.

Slip stitch

Back (right side)

Slip stitch the corner openings closed.

Fold the border fabric to the back and slip stitch it in place so that the stitches don't show on the front.

How to Stitch the Sashiko

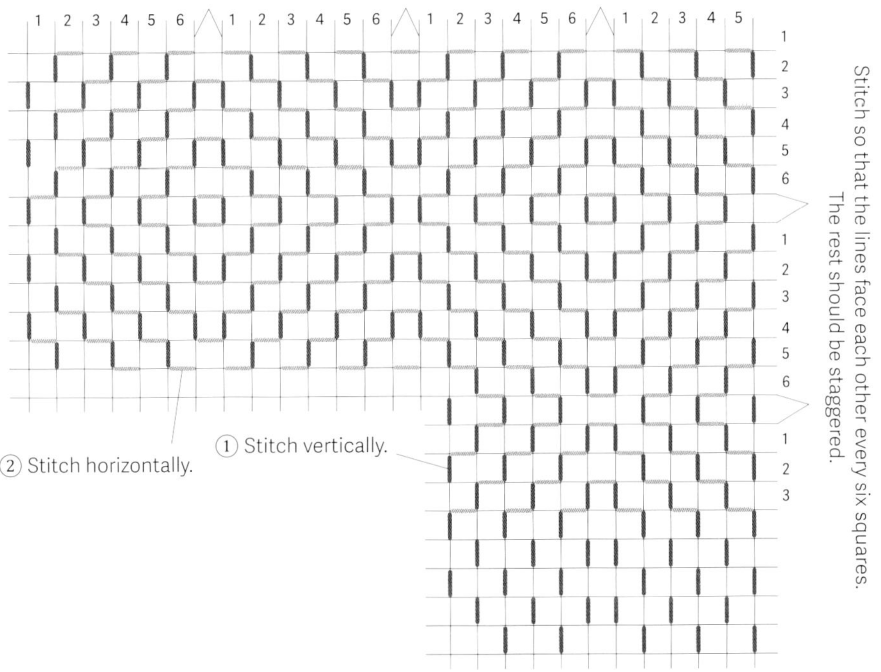

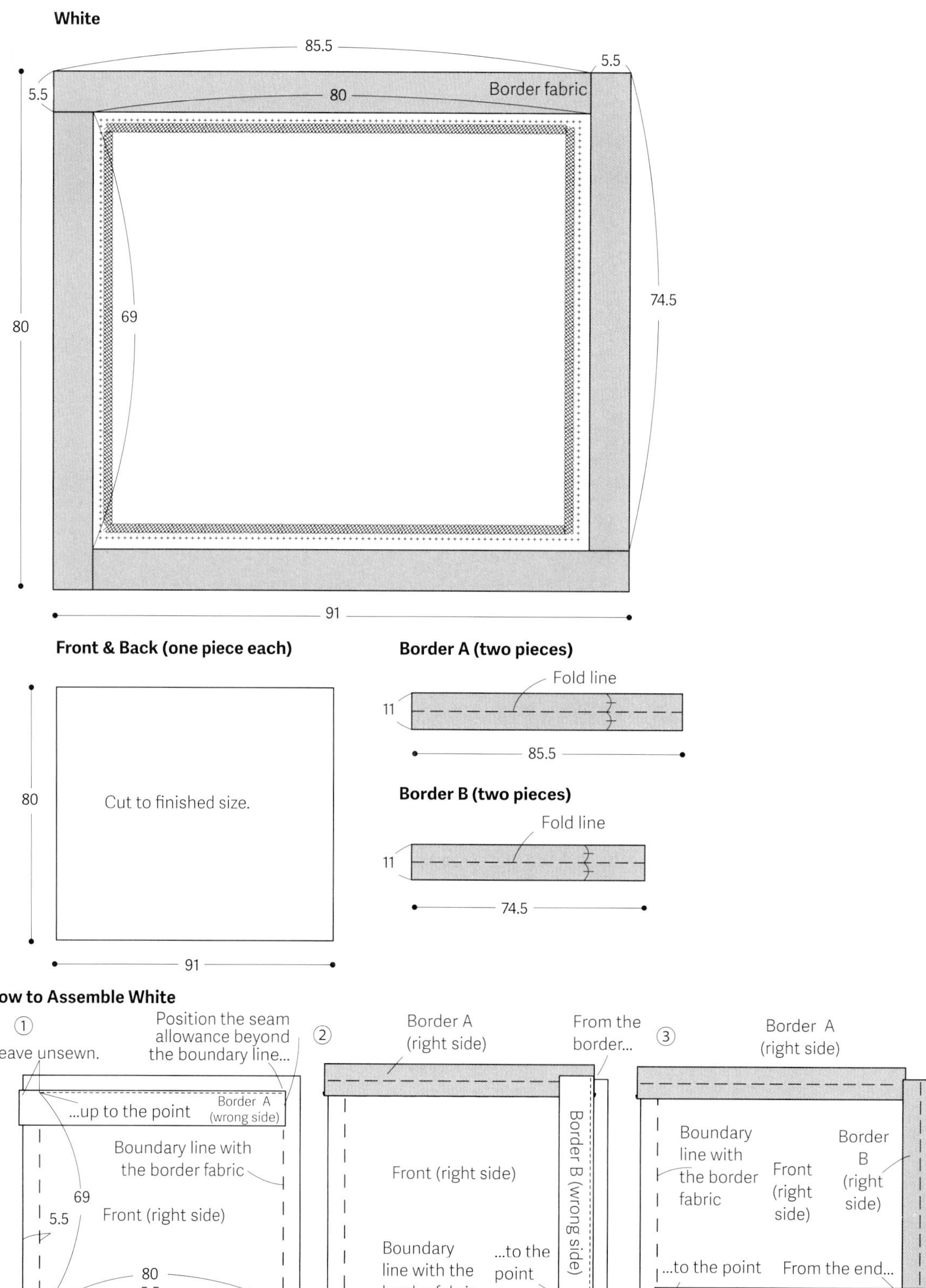

How to Assemble White

Layer the front and back with right sides facing out, layer border A with right sides together, and sew from point to point.

Fold the border (right side out), place border B right sides together on top, and sew from the edge to the marked point.

Fold the border (right side out), place border A right sides together on top, and sew from the edge to the marked point.

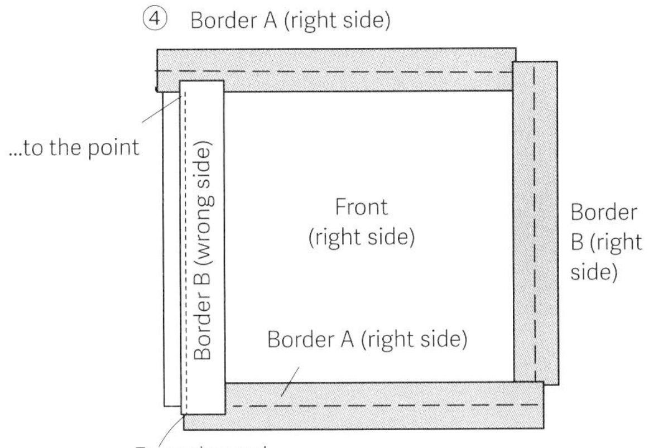

Fold the border (right side out), place border B right sides together on top, and sew from the edge to the marked point, making sure not to sew the end of the first border A together.

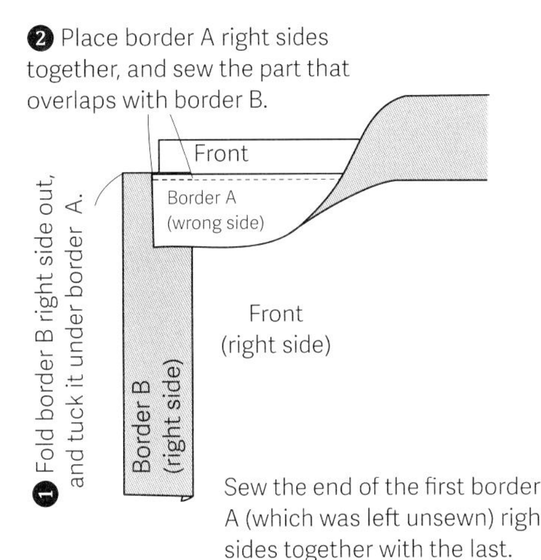

Sew the end of the first border A (which was left unsewn) right sides together with the last.

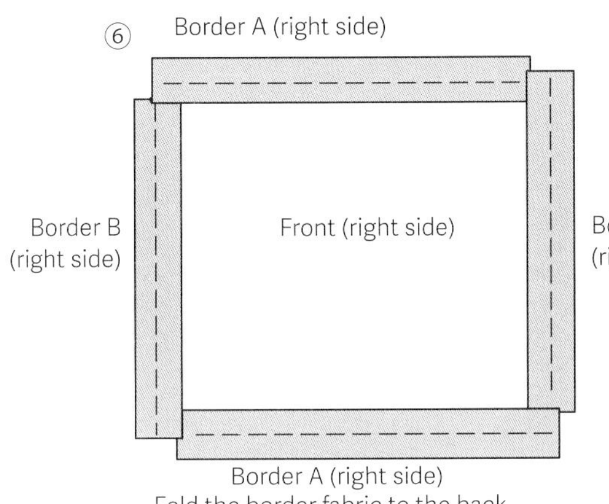

Fold the border fabric to the back.

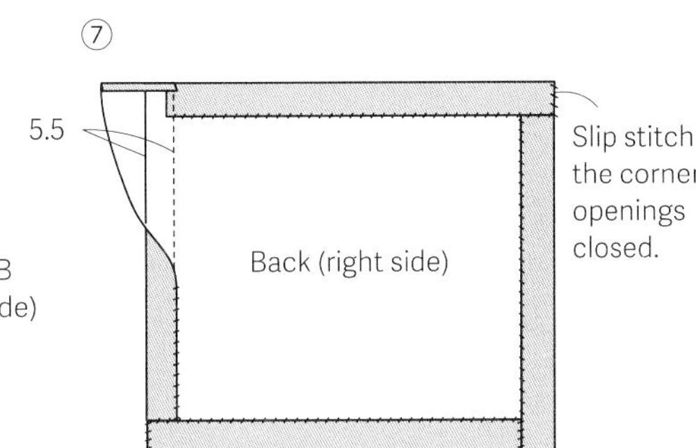

Slip stitch the borders to the back in order. At the corners, fold the seam allowance in as well to wrap the edge.

How to Stitch the Sashiko

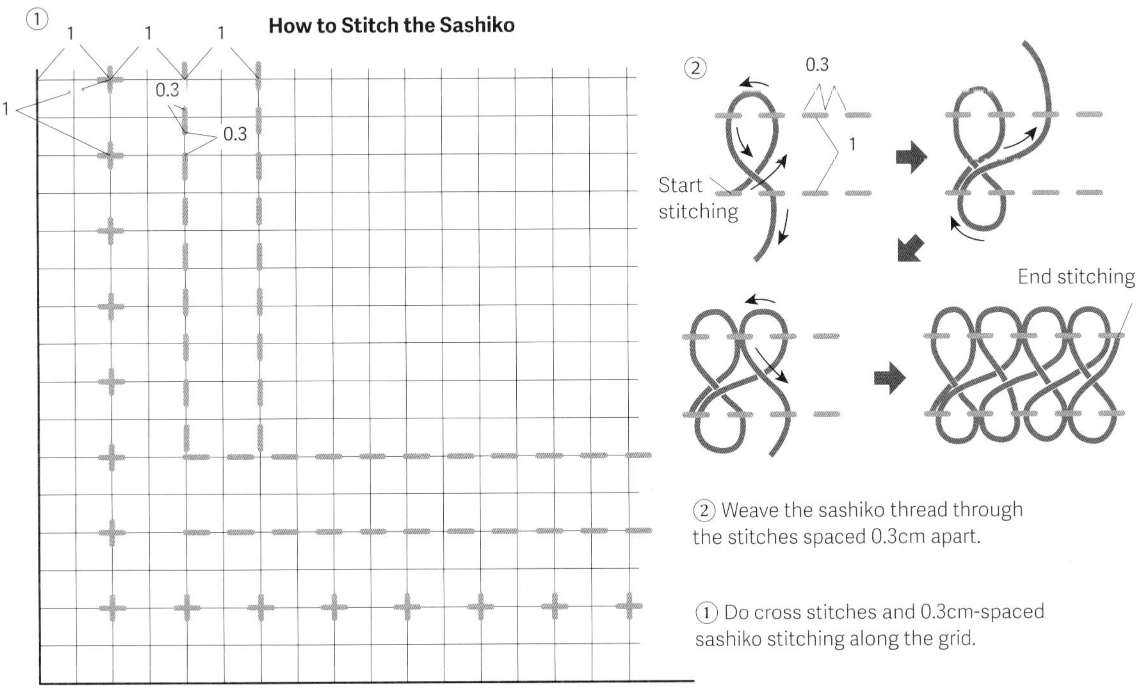

② Weave the sashiko thread through the stitches spaced 0.3cm apart.

① Do cross stitches and 0.3cm-spaced sashiko stitching along the grid.

INDEX